MINER

to

MILLIONAIRE

Front cover photo.

Author sitting in a stainless steel Model-T Ford car at the crossroad in the village of Ballenascarthy, which is approximately 40 miles south of Cork in southern Ireland.

It was donated by the descendants of William Ford who emigrated from there in December 1826.

Wuggles Publishing, Clydach, Swansea,
South Wales.

ISBN 978-1-904043-26-3

Grateful acknowledgements are given to the following for their help and support in the production of this book:

My Aunt Lilian, Julian Field, Brian Jones, Dafyd Saer, Viv Griffiths, Chris Thomas, David Evans, Mrs June Evans, Mr Francis John, Elwyn Williams, Mr Amos Powis, David Hillman, B. Richards, Ieuan Rees and the Neath Historical Society.

My thanks to you all.

Cy Williams, my father.

The inspiration for this book

WILLIAM CYRUS WILLIAMS

Cy' Williams was born in 1910 in Cefn Llan Cottages in Rhydyfro, a small village on the Pontardawe to Ammanford road. His father was a pickler in the Pontardawe galvanising works at that time. A pickler's job was to dip the metal sheets into a mixture to give them the galvanised finish. There were three elder brothers, Evan John, born in 1901, James Conwill in1906 and Ernest Tom in 1909. There had been two girls who had died very young Gladys Mary in 1900 and Helena Mary in 1904, Gladys after 6 weeks and Helena at almost 12 months (They are buried with their parents in St Peters church graveyard in Pontardawe.) All the children were baptised at St Peters Church, including the first little girl, who was baptised two days before she died.

In 1900 the family had lived in Old road Ynysmeudw a village just north of Pontardawe, but in 1905 on the advice of their doctor they moved to Rhydyfro as Evan had persistent breathing problems due to air pollution from the heavy industry in Pontardawe, Uncle Con, Uncle Ernest, my Father and my Aunt Lil were born in Rhydyfro. All four brothers were choirboys in St .Peters church at various times.

His parents had come from West Wales, father James Williams from Cio (Conwyl Caeo) and mother Mary Davies from Cilycwm, neighbouring villages in north Carmarthenshire.

Their mother was the strong character of the family, she made beautiful children's clothes which she sold to supplement the family income. She also made all kinds of cakes and preserves. Unfortunately she died of appendicitis in 1919.

Two years later their father remarried and their lives changed dramatically as the stepmother was no housewife or a good mother so the children had to do the cleaning.

During this time they had to sell off all their best clothes which their mother had made for them to pay the rent. Sometimes bailiffs would come and take some of the furniture, Aunt Lil remembers Father at 13 years old confronting the bailiffs to stop them taking some of their mother's favourite items. She also remembers him making money in a devious way by using a sieve propped up on one side by a stick with a length of string attached and food underneath it to attracted homing pigeons. When he caught one he would keep it for a few weeks so that it would be familiar with the area, he would then sell it and wait for its return then sell it to someone else to make more money. Another source of income he had was trapping moles, skinning them, drying out the skins and selling them to the local miners to use as pads for their elbows and knees. (they are very soft but hardwearing)

Sometimes his father and the older boys would put on thick socks over their boots to muffle their foot steps when collecting!! vegetables from local farmers' fields.

MY AUNT LIL

Rachel Lilly Williams was born in Rhydyfro in 1916 into a happy family of four brothers, for the first three years of her life things where good, but then her mother died when she was five years old. Her father then remarried and life changed dramatically. Her stepmother would make her do nearly all the housework including scrubbing the flagstone floors. As the four children in the second marriage where born she had to wash all their nappies as well. Because the extra income that her mother are brought into household, such as making children's clothes and selling preserved fruit, had now ceased, they frequently had to move house as they could not pay the rent. Their first move was to Abergorcy farm near Cwmgorse. Then Dynevor Villa in Penybanc, Brynmelin Farm in Penygroes and Llwyngarw Farm in Golden Grove.

When they were living near Cwmgorse she started going to school. Because she was so thin and bruised from the attentions of her stepmother the teacher would put her near the radiator to keep her warm. The school nurse would frequently take her home and admonish the stepmother for her treatment of the little girl. Every morning before lessons started each child had to show their hands to see if they were clean. If they were clean for a number of weeks a small badge would be awarded: Aunt Lil was awarded the badge on numerous occasions. When she was nine years old, one of her stepsisters who was three years old tried to swallow a badge but it got stuck in her throat and was choking her. The grown-ups didn't know what to do so Aunt Lil picked up the child, held her upside down and shook her until the badge came out, probably saving her life.

When they moved to Dynevor Villa in Penybanc near Ammanford she would have to go out every evening to sell a basket of eggs to make a shilling for her father's bus fare for the following day. He was working as an engine driver at the Duke colliery near Cwmgors, where they had previously lived. When she was fourteen, she went into service in the Dyffryn Stores in Ammanford to repay the ten pounds that her father had borrowed to buy a cow. She worked there for two years and then became a maid at solicitor's premises in Brynamman.

At about sixteen years of age she went to a clairvoyant who warned her that if she married someone with the same initials as herself (LW) there would be tragic consequences. She forgot about this prediction and married Leslie Williams, who tragically died in a roof fall at Tarenni colliery in the Swansea valley three years later.

She became very friendly with Tom Ellis James who she had met before, as he worked with her brother (my Father) Cyrus in Pwllbach as a collier. They were married in1939 and spent the first year in Rhiw Fawr then moved to Pentwyn Farm in Godrergraig, where their son John was born. After two years they moved down to Graig Road in Godrergraig before buying a house in Trebanos. Tom used to tease her that the first time he saw her she was scrubbing the floor in Cwmgorse.

MARRIAGE, MINING, MOTORCYCLES AND CARS

Father started working at the age of fourteen as a hewer's assistant. A hewer cuts the coal out of the coal seam; sometimes whilst lying on his side in the smaller seams in Pwll Bach, a drift mine up in the mountains at the top of the Swansea Valley. This type of mine was a tunnel cut as an incline (sometimes called a slant) sloping downwards into the earth to the coal seam. When he was promoted to a hewer He and Tom Ellis James (who later became his brother in law when he married Aunt Lil) held the record number of tons dug out in a shift. He later he became a haulier using a horse (which was often supplied by a local farmer) (see annexe on pit ponies) to pull the full drams from near the coalface to the bottom of the incline.

A Pit Pony at work

The roadways were not level as they had to follow the coal seam, which would either slope steadily or undulate. When going down a slope the haulier would put a sprag (a short piece of wood) through the spokes of one of the dram wheels to stop it turning, which slowed down the dram

The tunnels were cut with a groove along the centre of the roof to allow for the horse's head, which had a thick leather cover to protect it from the jagged rocks.

When arriving at the bottom of the incline he would disconnect the horse and then turn it around by putting its head down between the forelegs as the roadway was too narrow at this point to turn it around normally. He would then connect the drams to a cable that ran up to the surface, ring the bell, then attached the horse to the empty drams that came down as the full ones went up and take them to the various locations to be refilled by hewers assistants.

There was a signalling system used between the top and bottom of the incline. This consisted of bells at both ends, with the signal ready to pull up being three rings, for lowering down two rings and one ring to stop. The rope hauling up the drams would spin around as it took the strain of the loaded drams. One day, this was so violent that it caught my Father across his chest throwing him against the side of the tunnel and damaging his back (which needed surgery later).

At that time he was living with his brother Evan in Gwrhyd Isa farm up in the Gwrhyd Mountain to the west of the Swansea Valley, where he met mother when she visited her sister, May (Evan's wife).At that time she was a maid in Ty Coch house in Ystalyfera.

In 1933 they married and lived in Gwrhyd Isa at first then rented Pentwyn farm above Godrergraig in the Swansea Valley where I was born in 1936. The only source of heating there was the large fireplace in the kitchen with an oven on the left and a water tank on the right. This tank was the only source of constant hot water as the coal fire was never allowed to go out.

The Kitchen Fireplace

There was no electricity supply so paraffin lamps were used for lighting.

Paraffin Lamp

Father retired from mining shortly after I was born to concentrate on farming and buying and selling motorcycles.

In 1942 we moved to Pentreharne farm near Rhos where Father started trading in motor cars, small vans and pickup trucks. At one time we had eight cars on the farm (which my school friends doubted until I showed them). This was rare because so few people had motor cars at that time as they had to have coupons to get their petrol allocation.

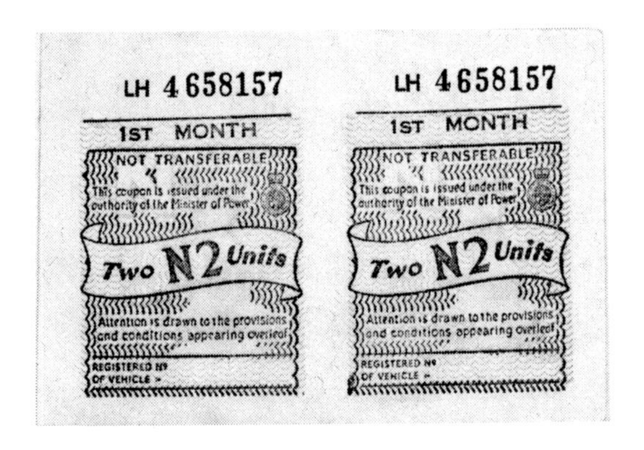

Petrol coupons

He also bought six ex-Army pickups (below).The Army nickname for them was the “Tilly” (short for Utility). 30,000 of these were made by various carmakers during the early part of the war, based on pre-war models. They were made by the Austin, Morris, Standard and Hillman car companies, and were used extensively until the American Jeeps arrived. The ones he bought were still in desert colours, (light brown and beige). We removed this paintwork using paint stripper and paraffin blowlamps then painted them in grey or blue before selling them to small builders and farmers, mainly in west Wales.

During that time he also bought ten burnt-out cars which had been destroyed in a garage fire in Pontardawe, when someone had lit a match while trying to siphon petrol out of one of them.

He bought all the pre-war taxis from a firm called Glamtax in Swansea: these cars were maroon coloured with a cream line running along both sides. The lines were removed and re-painted to match the rest of the car.

Most cars in those days had a 6-volt electrical system and were notoriously difficult to start in damp weather. An incident I remember from around this time was the first time I tried to drive a car. My Father was towing me down the farm road trying to start an old Ford 8. I kept braking too hard and snapping the tow rope; he got very angry and slammed the driver's door so hard he broke the window, making him angrier still.

He had a recurring back problem (from the coalmine accident) and had an operation at Morriston hospital in 1949 by having two discs removed.

During his stay there mother would visit him twice a day, going to Aunt Lil's (who lived in Godrergraig at that time) between each visit as it would have taken too long for her to go back to Rhos. Sometimes my brother Lyn would accompany her. My brother Lyn remembers Father lying in bed for days on an old door to try and ease the pain, and hobbling around the house on crutches made from two old sweeping brushes.

In 1950 he started attending meetings of a transport company called A.W. Thomas & son who were based in Tonna. A year later he became a director of that company. When the filling station was bought and renamed Stadium Service Garage he took control of it. (The name Stadium came from its location near the Greyhound Stadium across the railway behind the garage). Over the years he supervised the expansion of the site by having a new canopy erected over the petrol pumps and a new office/ tyre store built there.

Original filling station after bomb explosion.

He was a regular lunchtime customer in the Dorothy café on the Parade in Neath where he would dine with a number of his friends. As his wealth increased he would order a new Rolls Royce, keep it for a couple of months then sell it on at a profit. He was very active in the company until the early 1980s when he was taken ill and had to retire. He fought hard against the illness until he passed away in September 1986.

A WARTIME CHILDHOOD

I was born in September 1936 and named James Gethin Williams (James was mothers maiden name) in Pentwyn farm above the village of Godrergraig in the Swansea Valley. Some of my earliest memories are of walking over the hills to my Uncle Evan's farm escorted by our maid Lil Meredith to get fresh eggs and vegetables. While there we would help prepare hot baths for Uncle Evan and his son Cliff when they returned from the coal mine (before pit head baths). The water was heated in cauldrons over an open coal fire and would be poured into a galvanised tin bath in front of the fire. Sometimes a glass marble was put in the cauldron which rattled against the bottom to indicate when the water was boiling. The first pithead baths in South Wales were built at the Whyndam Colliery in the Ogmore Valley during the 1940s. Gas from the workings underground was used to fire the boiler for hot water in the showers.

Tin Bath

Another memory is looking down the valley and seeing Swansea being bombed during February 1941; the night sky was lit up by the explosions and fires.

Five Boys chocolate advertisement

On my way to and from school seeing advertising panels on a shop for Five Boys chocolate and Fyffe's bananas. I tasted neither until I was 10 years old.

Life then was one long adventure (I have the scars on my knees and face as reminders). The ones on my knees are from when I fell on a refuse tip onto some broken bottles. The one on my left cheek is from a barbed wire fence at the bottom of a steep field which I rode down on a small three wheeler bike with faulty brakes. The wire knocked me off the bike, which carried on over the edge of a quarry a few feet further on!

Three-wheeler bike

We moved to Pentreharne farm in 1942 which was about a mile southeast of Rhos, a village on the road between Neath and Pontardawe. I attended Rhos primary School where we sat at wooden desks with lids under which we would keep our satchels containing homework and exercise books. In front of the lid there was a hole where an inkwell was placed after being filled in the morning by one of the pupils. We would dip our metal-tipped pens in the ink to write, which could be a messy business if too much ink was on the nib of the pen.

This was when we were taught the three "Rs" - reading, writing and arithmetic. Arithmetic was drummed into us by repeating the times tables over and over again. These tables were on charts pinned to the walls of the classroom.

Writing was very difficult for me and I never conquered joined-up writing; my printing was once described as looking like a spider had crawled over the page. (and it still does).

A school inspector would visit once a month and ask one of us to spell the word because (b-e-c-a-u-s-e), that word is imprinted on my mind to this day.

My first taste of chocolate (in 1946) was in powdered form contained in tins that we took to school. On the two-mile walk back to the farm I would wet my finger and put it into the powder to taste it. (There wasn't very much left by the time I got home).

My first banana I shared with my brother Colin:
It was very smooth and a completely new taste to us.
During this time parcels were sent from America
Consisting mainly of bed sheets and children's clothing.
In some there were small jodhpurs (trousers) as worn by jo
Most boys wouldn't wear them as they
looked so comical.

The only time I received any physical punishment during my school days was when the bus that took us to woodwork classes in Trebanos every Wednesday afternoon didn't arrive so a few of us decided to walk there.

When we arrived in Trebanos we found the building locked so we walked back to Rhos to be confronted by the headmaster who gave us all two lashes of his cane across the palms of our left hands.

During the war there was no street lighting as the German aircraft could have used them during night time bombing raids as guides to their targets, so we played hide and seek, also "mob", in almost complete darkness during the winter evenings near the Co-op stores in the middle of Rhos. On summer evenings we would meet outside the school where the girls taught us boys how to dance. We would whistle the tunes and the girls taught us the steps of the foxtrot, quickstep and tango.

When we were older we would go by bus to Pontardawe on Wednesdays to the Moose hall to dance and Saturdays to the Rink dance hall, which is now a nightclub. The Rink was the main attraction with its large dance floor and a big coal fired stove at either end that we danced around to a six or eight piece band. As you can see by the dances we learned. This was before the Jive the Twist and Rock n' Roll. Everybody would move anticlockwise around the hall during all these dances.

I failed the eleven plus exam but a couple of years later passed a test to go to Pontardawe Technical College where I found the practical subjects more to my liking, as I had been working on my bicycle for years stripping it down almost every week and lubricating all the bearings.

When we moved to Fforest Goch in 1952 I would board the South Wales double-decker bus that ran between Neath and Ammanford every morning to go to Ponty Tech. The driver and I had a competition to see how fast I could run to jump on (clinging on to the pole on the back step) without him slowing down too much. All went well until one rainy morning when the pole was wet, when I grabbed the pole I began slipping down so he had to brake to allow me to swing on. We gave up the challenge after that.

An amusing incident from that time involved a very strict bus conductor who, on the way back from Ammanford, went upstairs and found that someone had been caught short and had left a deposit on the gangway. He stopped the bus and called the police. The very amused sergeant who arrived told him to scoop into a paper bag and put it in the lost luggage room to see if anybody claimed it. If it wasn't he could keep it.

During my time at the college I was usually third or fourth in the end of term exams, (usually let down by the cleanliness of my engineering drawing paper). I enjoyed my time there playing rugby and running on sports days. At one time we were asked what our favourite subject was; I said mine was mechanical engineering especially motor cars. The teacher then asked me to draw the fuel system of a typical car of that time; I did this and also explained how it worked to the astonishment of everyone in the classroom.

Having passed my driving test first time!! I became the driver for my four pals who I had become friendly with in college; Mike White, Brian York, Eric Jones and Brian Davies. I would pick them up in Pontardawe on Saturday evenings and drive up to Ystalyfera to the Smiths Watch and Clock Factory (the Tick-Tock) social club to play a few games of darts and drink a pint or two (no drink and drive laws then) before going on to the Regal dancehall in Ammanford via Brynamman. The road we used was narrow with a couple of humpback bridges along it. I delighted in going over them at high speed causing the rear passengers to hit their heads against the roof. (No safety belts). Mike worked in the machine shop at the Tick Tock and would make darts of a certain size and weight to suit each one of us.

On leaving college I started to work at Stadium Garage where my Father (known as Cy Williams) was a director. I was an apprentice mechanic for eighteen months until my call-up to do two years of National Service.

PENTREHARNE FARM

In 1942 we moved to Pentreharne (iron village) farm near Rhos where all the ground floor rooms had flagstone floors and a large open fire as in Pentwyn and no electricity supply for the first few years. The cold water tap was outside the back door where mother made us clean our teeth every morning, rain or shine. We each had different coloured toothpaste tin made by the Gibbs toothpaste company. (I'm very grateful to her for that as I still have most of my teeth at 75).

The only floor covering we had were rag mats that we made by using empty Hessian sacks that were laid flat and strips of cloth that had been cut to size (called thrums in some parts of the country) were inserted through the holes all across the bag using a special needle to make loops which were then cut to make the finished mat.

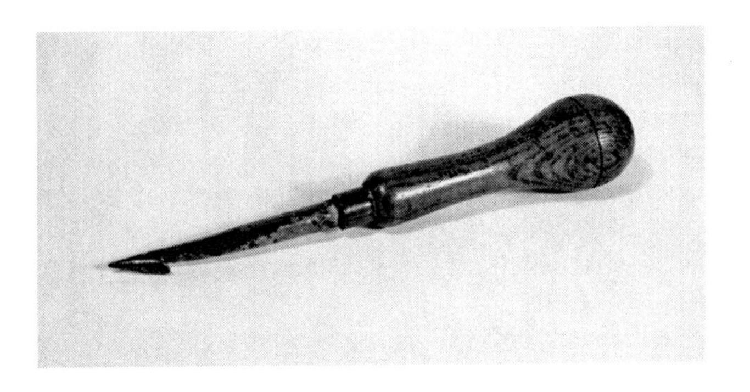

Needle for making rag mats

The pantry had thick stone slabs on which bacon was cured first by rubbing saltpetre into the bone sockets and the remainder covered with rock salt. When the hams were cured they would be hung on the beams above the fireplace and slices cut off them as required.

The only source of heating we had were coal fires, one in the kitchen with an oven on the left and a water container on the right side which was refilled every night and the fire stoked up to have warm water next morning. Every other room had a small fireplace which was only lit if someone was ill in that room or for special visitors in the parlour. The fireplace in the kitchen was made of iron which we polished with black lead so that all the metal had a dark grey shiny finish.

Washing day was always on a Monday when the water from the fireside boiler was poured into a large galvanised drum and the clothes, after being soaked and rubbed with a bar of soap, were pummelled with a washing dolly (posser) which was pushed up and down then to and fro to clean the clothes.

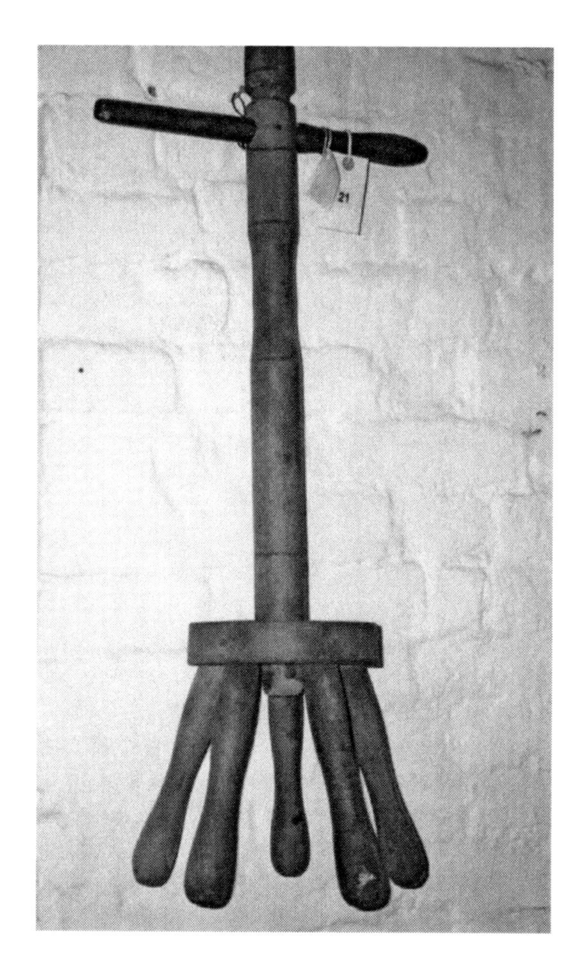

Wash Dolly (Posser)

Washboard and Mangle

The more stubborn stains were vigorously rubbed to and fro on a washboard; the type later used by skiffle groups. There were a few makes of soap, among which were Sunlight, Puritan, Lifebuoy, Fairy and Carbolic, the softest being Fairy and the hardest being Carbolic. There was also Pears, a much more refined soap which was used to wash our faces and in the bath. When washing powder was reintroduced, among the first were Persil and Rinso with many others following over the years. The first washing machine I remember mother using was an Acme with an electric motor to wash the clothes and a hand operated wringer on top with two rubber rollers.

The first all-electric washing machines we had with a spin drier was a Hoover Twin Tub made in Merthyr Tydfil. It was limited in size but was a great step forward in domestic washing. As the name indicates, it had two tubs; one for washing and the other for spin-drying. It became too small for us and was replaced by a Hotpoint machine with electric-powered rollers above the single tub. Care had to be taken when using this as a finger could be caught between them, which was very painful. Like all housewives in those days mother would preserve fruit mostly brought from aunt Ada's garden which was lovingly attended to by her father-in-law, or from our orchard. She would use Kilner jars which she filled with warmed fruit then screw on the top (early ones had screw tops) so that when the contents cooled it caused a vacuum in the jar to keep the contents fresh for months

The lighting we had was an oil lamp hung in the kitchen above the dining table and candles in holders to light our way to the other rooms. Whilst outside we had hurricane lamps to use in the cowshed and barns. These were fuelled with paraffin pressurised with a hand pump fixed to the base and burned inside a mantle which was protected from the weather by a glass cover.

Our wireless (radio) was powered by batteries (accumulators) made of thick glass and filled with acid which had to be carried to the Co-op stores in Rhos to be recharged every few weeks.

We would gather around the radio in the evenings to listen to "Dick Barton special agent" which was a fifteen-minute programme at a quarter to seven five days a week; also Green for Danger, Much Binding in the Marsh and The Billy Band Cotton Band Show.

Towards the end of the 1940s we had electric light installed, which was a great thrill for us having instant light at the flick of a switch.

There was no other power source such as three-pin sockets so the electric iron had to be plugged into the light socket hanging above the dining table in the kitchen using a two way adaptor so that the light bulb could be used at the same time. Hanging from the side of the lampshade was usually flypaper, which was a length of scented dark brown paper with glue on both sides to trap the flies; with a recommendation that it was renewed when three quarters of the surface was covered with dead flies. They were also killed by squirting Flit a D.D.T. fluid from a hand pump around the room.

The toilet was situated about fifty yards from the back door and consisted of a wooden shed built over a hole with a plank across it about two feet from the ground on which we sat. There were no toilet paper manufactured during the war so we would cut up newspapers or "The Farmers Weekly" magazine into six-inch (15cms) squares cut a hole near one corner, put a loop of string through and hang them on a nail on back of the door .A long-handled shovel was used to empty the contents which we then spread on the fields as manure. To save going that far at night there was a large ceramic pot under each bed (a goes-under).

Chamber Pot (A Goes-under)

Besides being a long way to go in the dark it was risky walking through the kitchen as the floor would be crawling with what we called 'black pads' - large black beetles that lived in the nooks and crannies around the fireplace and came out at night.

My youngest brother Lyn was born in 1945. His full name is Victor Lyn Williams, he was born on May the thirteenth; VE Day (Victory in Europe).

Below the farm there was a line of tall sycamore trees, one of which I would climb to keep a lookout for the government inspectors (Father called them spivs) who controlled the amount of livestock and crops on the farms. If I saw a strange car in the distance I would warn everyone to hide the cream, butter and any livestock that shouldn't have been there. One day an inspector caught us by surprise when there were four calves in the small cowshed which had a number of small rooms with access from one to the other. When Father and the inspector approached I was inside with the calves which I then moved from one room to another just before they entered it so I went around in a circle inside the building without being seen just ahead of them. These calves were destined to be slaughtered in a secluded wood on the farm along with cows which Father bought from various farms and bring them home in a horsebox being towed by a pre-war Austin 16 which had been fitted with a heavy duty rear axle to take the extra weight (its registration number was CWV 9)

One of the many encounters we had with the inspectors was when using the motorcycle and sidecar. I was sitting on half a salted pig in the sidecar when we were stopped by an inspector whilst fording the river Clydach near Tynycwm farm. While Father talked to him water started seeping in and I got a very wet bottom. We got away with it and proceeded to a butcher's shop in the Swansea valley.

Motorbike and sidecar

Another time I remember being in the sidecar was on the way home from Neath hospital after having my tonsils and adenoids removed. It was a rainy day so the top of the side car was closed over me, but I could see my Father through the side window on my right with mother sitting behind him as we were driving along the Bryncoch bypass.

I have another recollection of the bypass when, having bought a second-hand bicycle in Hills Cycles on Stockhams Corner in Neath, I wheeled the bike through the town across the old river bridge and up Rhyddings hill to the bypass where I mounted the bike and rode very slowly home. That first bike lasted for years travelling to and from Rhos along Tynycwm Road, which was then unmade with shallow potholes. I became so expert at avoiding the potholes that I could ride along it in the dark and miss each one. The next bike I had was a new Raleigh on which I spent many hours travelling around the area.

An incident which has saved me thousands of pounds over the years was when two friends and I acquired a packet of twenty Capstan full strength cigarettes and smoked them all between us down by the river bank. We were all so ill that none of us has smoked ever since.

We had twelve milking cows which I had to bring in from the fields after tea, (having walked home nearly two miles from school). After washing their udders I'd help to milk them by hand. (before we had the milking machine). The machine was powered by little single-cylinder Lister engine that drove a vacuum pump to draw the milk from the cows' teats. Two cows were usually milked at a time.

Milking machine

All the cows had different patterns of black and white that had to be recorded on special forms issued by the ministry of agriculture. They had the outline of both sides and the head of each cow on which was drawn their individual pattern. They were used to make sure we had the same ones each time the inspectors came around.

After milking we would use a separator to skim the cream off some of the milk for mother to make into butter, a process that my brothers and I assisted in by turning the churn. She would pay us half a crown (twenty five pence) a time. The skimmed milk would then be fed to the calves.

Butter Churn

Other livestock on the farm were a few sheep, some pigs and chickens. We had two large Shire horses. One was called Tiny the other Mabel.

Shire Horses

I well remember riding on the back of these horses in short trousers after they had been working the fields and their perspiration would burn the inside of my legs. We had to wear short trousers if we were under twelve years of age and men's trousers had no turn-ups, to save material for the war effort. The horses were used to pull various items around the farm including carts, ploughs harrows in the spring, and in the autumn mowers for cutting the hay and a reaper and binder for cutting and binding the corn, wheat and barley.

Reaper/binder.

When our first tractor arrived Father had all the horse drawn machinery converted to be towed behind the tractor by having towing brackets made at a local blacksmith.

This tractor was a Fordson N type manufactured in Ireland under an American license. The engine was started by turning the starting handle on the front and the engine speed controlled by a hand lever. It had two fuel tanks, a small one for petrol to start the engine from cold and a larger one for the TVO (tractor vaporising oil) which was used when the engine is warm. The TVO was cheaper and more readily available as petrol was still rationed at that time. The clutch and brake were controlled by one large pedal so when I started to drive it I was so small that I had to stand with both feet on this pedal with my left hand holding on to the steering wheel and my right under the edge of the rear mudguard to be able to press it down.

The first Tractor.

Our second tractor was a Fordson Major. This was a taller machine and the brake and clutch had separate pedals but still had a hand accelerator. This was also started with a starting handle and had a nasty habit of kicking back on the handle so we had to grip it with our thumb along side our hand to avoid having it dislocated. We later had an Allis Chalmers tractor which had a starter motor and had a gearbox like a car with which we could change gear while still moving and was used for lighter work around the farm.

Allis Chalmers tractor.

We had two servants; John Nielson, who worked the horses and tractors and did all the outside chores around the farm, and Lil Meredith who came with us from Pentwyn to help mother with the indoor work. Unfortunately Lil had to leave us after a short while as it was thought by the Ministry of Agriculture that the farm was too small to support two servants.

One of the hardest chores was helping John clean out the cowshed. This entailed loading the dung into a wheelbarrow and taking it down the farmyard and up a narrow plank onto the top of the dung heap without slipping off. To keep it on the plank we would put a mark on the front edge of the barrow directly above the wheel to guide us.

During the war we had Italian detainees working in the fields weeding between the rows of vegetables and helping with the harvest. These men were British citizens from Italian families that had been detained during the time we were at war with Italy. At the beginning of the conflict in 1940 a number of men from these families were sent by ship (The Arandora Star) to Canada, but the ship was sunk by a German U-boat off the west coast of Ireland with eight hundred and five people drowned (four hundred and seventy of these were Italians). Some of the few survivors were sent to Australia for the rest of the war. It was then decided to keep the rest of their countrymen here to help us in the war effort, working in various industries and on farms.

The Arandora Star steamship.

We had some colourful visitors to the farm. Romany gipsies would call to sell clothes pegs (dolly pegs) and baskets they had made and 'Johnny Onions' from Brittany selling strings of onions. which they carried hanging from the handlebars and sides of their bicycles both wearing their traditional clothes.

St David's day was a very memorable time in those days. My Aunt Ada and her children would come to visit us bringing a basket full of various sandwiches made with home baked bread and home grown fillings. These we would take up to a small wood on the hill above the farm where our mothers would gather some large stones into a circle and light a fire to boil water for tea and eat those delicious sandwiches.

I remember two very happy holidays we had in the early 50's. One was a week in a rented little cottage in Bracelet Bay near Mumbles. The other was with my uncle Dillwyn and Aunt Mary at Filton airfield near Bristol where my uncle was serving in the R.A.F. We saw the Bristol cars being tested and helped push the first single-engine jet fighter ever built in the UK which was the Gloucester Vampire out of its hangar. I remember thinking when I saw all the rivets holding the aluminium panels together that I wouldn't like to fly in it.

Gloucester Vampire jet fighter plane.

A treat we had in late summer was winberry (blue berry) tart made with the berries we had picked up on the mountainside, some of us using what we called a winberry comb, while the others had to use their fingers which were stained dark blue for a couple of days afterwards. We always looked forward to Saturday mornings when we would go down to Pontardawe to one of the three cinemas there. We had the choice of the Lyric, Public Hall or the Pavilion. We usually went to the Pavilion where we would watch the main film, a quarter of a hour of a cowboy film (with the next part being shown the following week), the latest news of the war by Gaumont British or Pathe and some items from the government warning us to make sure our blackout blinds were always closed tight and not to speak to strangers (all in black and white). On our way home we would call at a fish and chip shop to buy a bottle of green pop and a bag of chips to eat whilst walking home over Alltwen hill and through Rhos to the farm.

FFOREST GOCH

In 1952, after a number of improvements had been made to the house. we moved down to the main road in Fforest Goch, a little village between Bryncoch and Rhos on the Neath to Pontardawe road. The improvements that were made were new wooden floors instead of flagstones in all the down stairs rooms, electricity to the upstairs rooms and the conversion of one bedroom into a bathroom with a toilet. My brother Lyn remembers having a bath every night during the first week we were there and flushing the toilet just to watch the water disappear down the pan.

I remember the day we moved very well because when I came home from school, having walked a mile and a half from the bus stop, I found the farm deserted so I waited there a short while until my uncle Evan came to get me in his pre-war Opel car.

At that time, there was no sewage system in the village of Rhos. Every month a local farmer would go around the houses late at night with a horse and cart to empty all the outside toilet buckets that they would spread on a field (very smelly) near the main road until it was ready to be used as fertiliser in the Spring. The cart they used was especially built for the job. It was a cylindrical tank with a large hole at the top to tip in the buckets and would be emptied by turning the tank on its axis. They were called the midnight angels or 'Sweet Violets' by the villagers. In England they were called night- soil removers.

MY ARMY DAYS

After initial training at Honiton in Devon in the R.E.M.E. (Royal Electrical and Mechanical Engineers) I was posted to Germany. During the first year I was based in Kunsebeck, a small village near Bielefeld, at a large workshop where all kinds of army vehicles were repaired, from motorcycles to Chieftain Tanks. In the second year I was posted to a light anti-aircraft company outside Lippstat, where I looked after ten Ford Lorries that towed the anti-aircraft guns. Two Austin Champs (these were large jeeps with Rolls-Royce engines) and also the small engines fitted on each gun for charging the batteries to power their electric motors.

These small engines were started by winding a small rope around a pulley and then pulling it by a toggle at the end of the rope. They were very temperamental, especially in damp weather when we were out on manoeuvres. We would remove the spark plug from the engine and warm it up in the flames of a small fire we lit. Sometimes our hands would be very painful and bleeding after pulling the rope so many times.

I have some fond memories of my time in the army. One was the first time I tasted Coca-Cola, while on a two week skiing course, (I still remember the taste of that first bottle).

Another highlight was having been in the American Zone on manoeuvres at that time there were four zones in Germany, French, British, American and Russian, in a pine forest, for two weeks without access to a bath or shower. What a luxury that first shower was back in our barracks, washing off all the grime and pine needles. An amusing yet painful incident to some was when someone cleaning the toilets in our accommodation block-rubbed caustic soda on the seats causing a number of my colleges' severe burns on their posteriors.

During that second year I joined a music group entertaining the officers of the regiment on a monthly basis. That's when my interest in singing began, with " Sixteen tons," Old Man River" and "On the Street Were You Live" as my solos. I was promoted to Corporal First Class with a promise of becoming a sergeant if I signed on for a further few years but I decided not to take up the offer and returned to Civvy Street.

BACK TO THE GARAGE

I rejoined the garage in 1957 and continued training as a mechanic until the early 60s when Father rented the Dyffryn Arms filling station near Bryncoch, where I worked for a number of years doing small repairs on cars and motorcycles and serving petrol from 8 am until 6 pm.

The filling station was unique because after 6 pm customers would have to press a button on one of the canopy support pillars to activate a bell in the Dyffryn Arms where Father regularly played cards with some friends, (Ken the Butch) a butcher with a stall in Neath market, (Dai the Mill) as he lived in the Mill house across the road from the pub, and also Bill Burdett, who's family now runs The Continental Garage in Abercrave

Dyffryn Arms filling station

Bill told me a story about the landlady's poodle which was given bones by the regular drinkers on Friday nights. They put them near the coal-fired stove in the centre of the bar floor. One night Tom "flat wheels" (he drove a steamroller for the council) came in late and when he saw the bones said: 'that bloke must have waited a long time for his pint.' Another story Bill recalls is about John Gardiner who played cards with the group occasionally and would call everything "cowing this and that" in every sentence. Father got fed up with this one night so while John was in the toilet he persuaded Ada the barmaid to put a glass of milk on the bar for John, who on his return at first protested at this, but saw the funny side and rarely used that word after that. Another of Bill's recollections is of one stormy Saturday afternoon one winter Father telephoned his friends asking them to meet at the pub to watch a Welsh international rugby game. When they arrived the wind was so strong the TV aerial clamped the pub chimney was being moved about, so Father asked for a volunteer to go up on the roof to hold the aerial steady. Sat in the corner was Dai Iago who would do anything for a pint or two. Father persuaded him to go up onto the roof where he stayed until the end of the match being supplied with a pint of his favourite brew every half hour. He also told me about the night when the customers in the pub were reluctant to leave (licensing hours were 6 pm till 10pm every evening) so Father got Ada the barmaid to start a conga line that would take them all outside so he could close the doors behind them, but they closed them behind her instead and carried on drinking. Saturday evenings were very popular in the 'Duff'. Bill Bevan would go along to play his banjo, Father would sing 'Don't laugh at me 'cause I'm a fool' made famous by Norman Wisdom. while Mrs Booth would sing "Sailor, stop your roving".

One of my many memories of that time is of my father-in-law, Ogwyn Jones, calling in with his 1938 Morris

Eight, wondering why there were sparks running along the petrol pipe from the engine to the body of the car, it turned out that an earth strap had broken between the engine and the bodywork and the only way that the electric current could go back to the earth side of the battery was through the metal braiding around the petrol pipe. I fitted a new earth strap which cured the problem.

After a couple of years it was decided the filling station was too busy for me to run on my own, but not profitable enough to support another person, so I returned to Skewen where I became foreman and subsequently workshop manager in the Lucy Road. workshops. In 1965 I became a director of the parent company Stadium Transport (Skewen) limited.

I remained a director until 2002 when I sold my shares to my brother Lyn.

I carried on working part-time at the garage until February 2009

MY FAMILY LIFE

I was married in May 1958 to Mary Elizabeth Jones (Betty) Later that year we moved to a house in Crymlyn Road in Skewen which had once been a sub post office. The telephone box was still in front outside the bay window and a letter box was in one of the front gate pillars. All the interior woodwork was painted in beige undercoat, (doors, window frames, skirting boards and staircase) and the front room walls still had the marks where the shelves had been. Our first pieces of furniture were all second-hand bought from Ken's shop on the Croft in Neath.

Our first child was born two years later. We named him Cyrus Gerwyn; Cyrus after my Father. Three years on Mary Susan, Mary after mother, came into the world then eight years later Michael Alun.

When Alun was born, number 119 became too small so later that year (1971) we moved to 91 Crymlyn Rd, from where Gerwyn and Susan were married, and when old enough Alun also moved out. Betty and I stayed there until 1999 when we moved to Clydach.

My eldest son Gerwyn married Wendy Baggride and has two children Nicola and David.

Nicola has a little girl Stephanie so I'm now a great grandfather.

My daughter Susan was also married and has two children Gavin and Julia Lynsey.

MY SOCIAL LIFE

On this side of my life I have served on various committees starting with the Bryncoch rugby club on the entertainments committee where Dennis Davies (Den the Pen) and I would book artists for the Saturday night concerts. We'd get them through Bert Veal, a theatrical agent in Alfred Street, Neath, or from talent shows that we attended around the area.

One of the most famous artists we engaged was Alan Davies, who had won the Opportunity Knocks competition on TV for seven weeks in 1965.

The Saturday night shows were always very well attended. We would start Bingo at 7.30 pm after I had sold the tickets. I then sat next to the caller, usually Dennis, handing him the numbered discs out of a bag (no machines then) and finally shouting back the numbers for the winning line or full house.

At 8 0 pm our compere, Ron Hughes, would start the concert by introducing the organist for the night, who played a few tunes on the organ (which we had bought from the Colliers Arms in Clydach). He would then introduce the artist for the night, who did about a hour and was usually a singer or a comedian. The night ended with dancing to music played on the organ.

Some of the most enjoyable trips we had during that time were to the Scotland v Wales rugby matches in Edinburgh. Every other year, usually starting on Thursday mornings, we would assemble at Neath railway station. The coach next to the guard's van was reserved for us and the beer barrels, beer cans and the gas cylinders were loaded into the guard's van. The beer was usually flowing before we reached Pyle (free to us as we had paid for it in our trip money). On reaching Waverly railway station in Edinburgh that evening the remaining beer and equipment were stored in the left luggage office until Sunday morning, when everything would be loaded back on the train We would enjoy our journey home selling any excess beer to others and the money made invested towards the next trip.

During that time the Aberfan disaster happened when the huge, waterlogged coal tip above the village slid down the mountain killing a hundred and sixteen schoolchildren, their teachers and a number of residents.

When this was announced that evening in the club a number of the players volunteered to go there and spent several days and nights digging out the area.

One of the members of the club who worked for the Sunblest bakery in Neath Abbey went into work especially to make pasties and pies that were shipped by the lorry load to the scene of the disaster over the next couple of weeks to feed the hundreds of people clearing the coal waste and ruined buildings.

When the drink- drive law was introduced in 1967 it had a profound effect on clubs and public houses which were located outside a village or town. In the Bryncoch club the attendance on Saturday nights dropped by over a half and became too costly to hold the concerts. I resigned from the committee there and joined the social section of the Skewen rugby club, which was at the bottom of my garden. Harry Tristham was chairman and Mr and Mrs. Wolf were steward and stewardess at that time.

It was at this club Bonnie Tyler was discovered by Bert Veal (the agent we used here also) when she was singing in a charity show.

Also it was here I first met Max Boyce, who was at the beginning of his carrier and was still working in the Metal Box factory as an electrician. (The Metal Box factory made tins mainly for the food industry and was situated in the Melyn area of Neath.)

A few years later I was voted onto the management committee of Neath rugby club, where I again met Max during the visit of a Japanese rugby team when he sang "You go You go You go Shee, Me Welsh Speaking Japanee". I recently met Max when he was guest artist at fiftieth anniversary concert of the Bridgend Male Voice Choir in Porthcawl when I reminded him of our previous encounters. Incidentally, at the time of writing, Max is a patron of the Bridgend choir.

In the1988-89 season the Neath Rugby team were at their best scoring a world record number of points and the world record number of tries scored in a season.

During those years Ken Davies and I would clean the stands and surrounding areas, usually on Sundays, often with the help of a number of young men from the Farm School which was a detention centre in Neath. On one Sunday day I found a nail file under a seat in the main stand which I still use today.

Over the years I have been involved in various other committees including being chairman of the Swansea jalopy club where we raced around a rough field in old cars that had been modified by having all the interior upholstery (except the driver's seat) and windows removed and a roll cage built inside. The first field was near Morriston Hospital and later the abandoned racecourse in Fforestfach to the west of Swansea.

I was President of the Neath and Briton Ferry Chamber of Commerce until it amalgamated with others in the area to form The West Wales Chamber of Commerce.

I became chairman of Neath constituency Conservative Party for a number of years and campaigned against Peter Hain a few times.

When European money was available under the Objective One Scheme, various committees were formed in Swansea consisting of representatives from the public, private and voluntary sectors. I was appointed to the Swansea Management Committee from the private sector for processing the applications;

I also chaired one of the sub-committees where the applicants had to produce a convincing case for us to recommend to go forward to the management committee.

I was chairman of the Retail Motor Industry Federation for the South Wales and West Country region until early 2009.

I was chairman of the South Wales region of the Federation of Small Businesses for twelve years during which a number of us reinvigorated the F.S.B. in the region with a large increase in membership which, according to the Federation rules, meant we had to form branch committees to cope with the problems of the day to day running of all these businesses. The branches for our region are South East Wales, Powys, Swansea Bay, Carmarthen, Pembroke and Ceredigion. When the Swansea Bay committee was formed I became chairman and was reappointed for 11 years until I stepped down in 2010.

MY SINGING CAREER

As I mentioned earlier, I started singing in the army during my national service and sang then only occasionally until I joined the Rhos Cwm Tawe Male Voice Choir nearly twenty years later in June 1975, six weeks before we appeared on TV after winning our category at the National Eisteddfod in Criccieth. I was appointed chairman of the choir for a number of years, during which time we toured various countries in Europe and the USA, which included Birmingham in Alabama where we sang in the church where five girls had been killed by a bomb the Klu Klux Clan had set. A window which was bought by donations by the people of South Wales is fitted into the wall where the explosion occurred and is called the Welsh Window.

In 1982, after the choir sang at the Thousand Voices concert in the Albert Hall in London, a large choir was formed called The South Wales Male Voice Choir (Cor Miebion De Cymru) which toured the north east of the USA the following year. We sang four concerts in the Heinz Hall in Pittsburgh with the Pittsburgh Philharmonic orchestra, and because of the huge demand for tickets we had to sing an extra concert in a nearby sports hall. During that tour we also sang in Baltimore and Buffalo and visited Washington where we formed the American flag while standing on the steps of Capital Hill wearing red, white and blue jumpers. I stayed with that choir for quite a few years touring various parts of the UK, North America and Europe.

I joined the Neath male choir (which was then called the Melyncrythan and based at 'Paddies' club in the Melyn). In 2005 I became a member of the Bridgend Male Choir, where I sing solos in their concerts. In 2007 I left the Rhos Cwmtawe Male Choir, which later disbanded. At the time of writing I am still singing with Neath and Bridgend choirs.

My other hobbies include buying and selling old records, record players, radios, cine cameras and projectors; also sewing machines. The latter I take to a charity shop in Ystradgynlais who send them to be checked over and repaired if necessary before being sent to various countries in Africa.

SOME OF SKEWEN'S WELL-KNOWN CHARACTERS.

Before I describe these people I'd like to share some of the stories on how Skewen and Coedffranc got their names. One version of Skewen says that it came from the time when monks wearing white robes escorted Saint Francis from Briton Ferry where he had come ashore to the Neath Abbey Monastery. The old name is Sciwen, which in ancient Welsh apparently means 'white robe'. Coedffranc again seems to have come from that same visit and means Franks or Francis's wood.

One of the many characters living in Lucy Road was Lew Lewis. He lived with his wife Blodwen (Blod) and son Valden at Number eight. One of Lew's jobs was to control the decoy (hare) the dogs chased around the track in the greyhound stadium. It was driven around by an electric motor powered by an ancient battery system which he topped up with acid before every race meeting.

The battery, motor and the large control lever were housed in a small metal shed where during the races the heat from the motor and the fumes from the acid must have been overpowering. He told his nephew Francis John (FJs Hairdressers) stories of the history of the track. One was that in the early twentieth century a mini-circus with a number of cheetahs used to tour the country and would call at Skewen and race these beautiful cats around the track. Another was on various occasions greyhounds would race over hurdles with small monkeys sitting on little saddles tied to their backs.

Mr and Mrs. Powys, who live in Number 2 Dynevor Place, also recall seeing horse trotting. These are races where the horses pull a lightweight two-wheeled buggy carrying the jockey around the track. Mrs Powys remembers the time when the large circus came through the village she would give crusts from a special basket to the elephants as they walked by. She says that one day one lifted its trunk up high to receive the food, which really scared her.

At home, Lew had a shed at the top of the garden near the stream where he would rear poultry (chickens and ducks) which he had hatched in the oven alongside the fireplace in his kitchen. After one very heavy night of rain he found the day-old chicks all floating on the water in the shed. On hearing of his predicament his neighbours produced a large bowl each with a towel in the bottom and took the bedraggled bundles of fluff into their homes and set them near their fires to dry out. They all survived, luckily.

In another shed Lew had a very large glass bottle encased in straw in a metal mesh container from which he would dispense measures of paraffin, and from the house he and Blod used to sell pop.

Blod made pasties and sandwiches which she sold in a little shop at the greyhound stadium on race nights. The pasties she made were a speciality and would be sold out very quickly. Her nephew Francis has re-discovered the recipe recently and is thinking of reintroducing them.

Others who lived on Lucy Road were Bryn Davies in Number 10, who was an undertaker, assembled coffins in a big black shed below the house. Bryn was a very good boxer and fought for a Welsh title. Next door lived Elvet Davies a prolific singer, who won numerous competitions. Harold Lewis was another character who bred canaries. Next door to him lived Bill Cook who had a barber's shop on New Road where there is car park now in front of where Thomas the ironmongers used to be. Alongside Bill Cook's, with the doorway on Queens Road, was a bookmakers shop run by Phil Owen. This had originally opened in 1875 to sell fruit and vegetables by the Philips family and was the first to sell bananas in this area. Their son bought a small farm in Bryncoch near the Main colliery (now the rugby club) and opened a flower nursery there which their grandson recently closed due to ill health. In the furthest house on the right in Lucy Road (now abandoned) lived Aida Griffiths an eccentric lady who had a shop where the Texaco filling station is now. She could carry a sack of potatoes under each arm and handle any man who upset her.

Other well known individuals in the area were Tommy George, a coal merchant who lived in Number 4 Sidings Terrace and had a double garage facing onto Lucy Rd; one for his lorry and the other for his car. Others living in Sidings Terrace were Sammy Jarvis in Number 15, who sold fish and chips. Number 17, Mr. and Mrs. Llewellyn. Mr Llewellyn was an excellent sign writer and did a lot of work for Stadium Transport.

In Number 18 lived Elwyn Williams who recalled when driving home from Neath one evening in the little mini car he had bought from Stadium Garage, he saw three of his friends walking along so he offered them a lift to Skewen. On arriving at the Queens Hotel in Skewen they asked him to join them for a pint but he declined as he had just passed his driving test, so they lifted the mini onto the front patio of the pub where they left it until he agreed to have a drink.

Norman Williams (Norman the Oil) who, like his father before him, had a horse and cart to deliver paraffin, various utensils and small items such as wicks and mantles for the paraffin lamps to the households around the area, (he had a van in the latter years) and lived in Dynevor Place on the corner of Graig Rd. Behind the house stood a large garage where he kept all his wares and the cart, (later the van). Also in Graig Rd, Mrs Ware had a shop in her bungalow (arrowed in photo of brickworks, page 59) where the employees of the brickworks would purchase cigarettes and snacks.

Number 2 Brookfield Drive (once called Railway Terrace) lived Handel Edwards, who's trade was a plasterer but he became very famous for his wooden sculptures. He had various exhibitions around the country and a film made by S4C of three of his largest examples, The Miners Kitchen, which is in a museum in Ireland, that took him three years to make, The Angel, which has biblical scenes set in it and is on display in the Holy Trinity Church in Llandudno, that took him five years to make and the third is a scene from Oliver Twist showing Oliver holding his bowl when asking for more on a plinth standing in front of various depictions from Charles Dickens' book of that name. This third sculpture was in his front room forming the mantlepiece around the fireplace. Yet another worker in the village was called 'Chucks' because his job was to add sugar by "chucking it" into the vat in the Evans Bevan brewery in Cadaxton.

A.W.THOMAS & SON (TONNA) LTD.

This company was the forerunner of Stadium Transport Skewen Ltd and was based in Tonna, a village just north of Neath. It had been registered as a company in 1947 and had contracts to supply red ash from various tips (these were coal tips that had been on fire) in the area to local building companies as hardcore to fill in foundations of buildings and roads.

In 1949 a contract was signed with a company expanding the Llandarcy oil refinery near Skewen.It was called The Anglo Persian refinery in the 1920s—30s. During WW2 it was taken over by the Government and was then called the National Oil Refinery and known locally as the N.O.R. After the war it reverted to BP and became known as the Llandarcy refinery. The contract A.W.T. had was to prepare the groundwork for this very large expansion and so a large number of lorries and various machines were purchased and hired to clear the land and dig the foundations for the storage tanks and the specialist processing plants. During that time they expanded the lorry fleet to nearly seventy (most of them for site work and a varied selection of British, Canadian and American ex- military tippers and long wheelbase).

In 1950 Mr. Cy Williams became involved in the company, which during the next three years had contracts with G Walker and Slater, and William Press in the Llandarcy refinery. Outside contracts were also obtained with Evans Bevan delivering bricks from the Skewen and Cwmavon brickworks and the Cleveland Bridge company to supply hard-core for the construction of the M4 motorway embankments with a million tonnes to be supplied for the Earlswood to Lon-Las stretch and three quarters of a million tonnes for the Briton Ferry to Aberavon section.

A large number of subcontractors were engaged at this time to fulfil this enormous task.

In July 1953 the registered office was moved from Tonna to a yard behind the Lucy Road workshops in Skewen. Earlier that year the company had secured a maintenance contract for the railways and buildings in the Albion steelworks in Briton Ferry. When the Llandarcy contract ended the following year all the vehicles, machines and the site office were moved to Briton Ferry. A year later the contract at the Albion was extended to include all the roads in and around the works.

I worked night shifts there driving a small dumper truck to remove the still warm brick lining from inside the K furnace during its annual shutdown and also on Sundays helping to remove scaling from the pits below the rolling mills (the outer skin that fell off the steel as it cooled while being rolled).

During the time the company was based in Briton Ferry the hardcore (steel making waste material) around the steelworks was transported to the site of the B.P. Chemicals complex at Baglan (about a mile to the east) to form the foundation for the buildings and the railway network (which we maintained for years after the completion of the works). Hardcore was also delivered to form the base of the

M.E. Edwards gas plant alongside the westbound carriageway of the M4 between the new Briton Ferry Bridge and Llandarcy Junction 43.

An accident book was kept at the Briton Ferry office in which various amusing incidents were reported. (Original spelling):

1) I was loading girders on to the lorry when one slipped and hit me in the testicles.

2) Whilst lifting oxygen bottle, tripped causing it to strike me in the privates.

3) Forgot to put handbrake on lorry when securing tail board, it rolled back over my left foot had x-ray in Neath general hospital and returned to work.

In June 1955, A. W. Thomas and his son Howard retired from the business leaving Cyrus Williams, J. D. Turner and Ifor Jones as directors of the company. The following year J D Turner resigned as director. To secure more "B" licenses (see annexe 1) four lorries were purchased from Richard Bros of Crynant.

The company's name was changed to Stadium Transport (Skewen) Ltd in 1955.

STADIUM TRANSPORT

The company operated from Briton Ferry until the closure of the steelworks in late 1978 when a yard and workshops were purchased from Monarch Transport located in Neath Abbey (known locally as Rewbridge's yard).

The company carried on with the BP Baglan contract maintaining the railways within the Chemical complex and other small jobs. In 1985 the Metal Box Company in Neath was another customer where the roads and playing fields were maintained, the nearby canal banks, spillways and lagoons kept in good order. Also production machines moved around within the buildings when different products were made (these were moved by using a special mobile crane called an Iron Fairy that was low enough to go into various places). Other contracts included British Rail maintaining various parts of the Swansea to Paddington main line and also extinguishing a fire in the embankment at Landore. The embankment fire was deep in the hard core and because the railway could not be closed it took months of work pumping in chemicals to finally extinguish it. We had a contract with the local lighthouse company to take oil out to the Mumbles light twice a year in 45-gallon drums at very low tides and to take maintenance crews out to the light at the entrance to the river Neath in Briton Ferry (this second job was very hazardous because the sand was very soft in some places and the first attempt failed so an ex-army four wheel drive lorry that had been in the Sahara desert during the 1939-45 war got the job done.

Iron Fairy

An ironic thing happened in the mid-1980s when an agreement was signed for the demolition of some of the storage tanks and other buildings that the company had helped build in the1950s in the Llandarcy refinery. Over the next few years as the lorries and machines grew too old to be economically repaired the company was downsized and the Neath Abbey yard sold leaving only the BP Chemical and Metal Box contracts which were eventually relinquished leaving only the office in Skewen as the parent company of the garage.

STADIUM GARAGE

View of petrol station after bomb blast.

This property in Dynevor Place was bought from Mr W. Butler in 1952 by A.W.Thomas & Son for £1,800, to supply petrol for the lorries that were working in Llandarcy during the expansion of the oil refinery. It was named Stadium Garage after the Greyhound Stadium which was across the railway line behind it. There were four different makes of petrol sold at the garage for the first few years

BP, Shellmex, Power and National Benzole, and was the only filling station open on Sundays during that time.

I started working there in July 1953 as an apprentice mechanic in the workshop attached to the filling station. During that time I had an accident when I fell off a vehicle lift spraining my right wrist and cutting my lower jaw. The young nurse in the casualty unit at Neath hospital was quite annoyed with me because I was wearing overalls which she had to cut off because my wrist was too swollen for it to be removed in one piece.

We became retail dealers selling new Ford, Standard and Triumph cars; also second-hand cars and vans of all makes. At that time new cars could only be taxed in Greyfriars Road in Cardiff near the New Theatre. (Road tax in the U.K. was first introduced for horse drawn hackney carriages in 1637). One of my jobs was to go to Cardiff on the A48 road which then had three lanes in some places and was very dangerous because the middle lane was for overtaking in either direction. I had a few close shaves on that road.

On the Skewen side of the filling station there were two small buildings, the Cosy Cafe and the Enterprise Stores.

The Cosey Cafe opposite the Travellers Well. Beatrice Amyes

Cosy Cafe

The Cosy Cafe first came into being, in 1954, when it was bought by Mr. Arthur Grey from The British Transport Company then sold in the same year to Mrs E Thomas and then four years later to Mrs Leila Hoare the daughter of Mr Arthur Thomas, one of the directors of A.W.Thomas & son. She in turn sold it on to Mr and Mrs Pyle, and then in June 1965 it was bought by Stadium Transport and demolished.

The Enterprise Stores started at around the same time. (1954) when Mrs Olive Tallamy bought it from British Transport. Four years later she sold it to Mrs Frances Ada Williams. In1964 it was bought by Mr W A Hughes who a year later sold it to Stadium Transport when it suffered the same fate as the Cosy Café

The cleared the ground was then used to house three large underground tanks to store the three grades of petrol being supplied by BP (who were the only suppliers since they had contributed towards the cost of the new canopy and pumps).

New petrol station

The three were regular 91 octane, blend 95 octane and super 99 octane. The different grades were used according to the type of engine fitted. The older vehicles would use the 91 octane, as the engines had low compression, whereas the more modern ones and sports cars would use a higher octane. The word "octane" comes from the fact that petroleum has eight hydrocarbons in its composition "Oct" meaning eight and "ane" to make it a complete word. This was all long before the air pollution issues became relevant and unleaded petrol was introduced.

The first office at the filling station was the body of an ex Royal Air Force lorry which had originally been painted in black and white squares and had been used at the end of the runway on airfields to direct aircraft landing and taking off during WW2. The chassis and cab was used as our first Breakdown truck.

The first breakdown truck.

The first manager of Stadium garage was Mr. George Bees. In 1959 Mrs Jean Powell became his secretary and remained with the company in various capacities until 2009. Mrs. Sylvia Michael was secretary from 1970 until 1994.

The first Petrol attendant was George Williams, who lived across the road, as there was no self-service until 1961. He would, if asked, put a shot of Red X (Called Upper Cylinder Lubricant) at a penny a time into the fuel tank before the petrol. This gave additional lubrication to the top of the engine giving it more power and keeping the valves and piston free from carbon deposits. The hand-held pump had a nozzle that looked similar to a part of the male anatomy and many jokes were made about it.

Another smaller mobile pump dispensed a mixture of special oil and petrol for use in two-stroke motor cycles, scooters and cars. It was used extensively until the cars were discontinued in this country due to the air pollution problems they allegedly caused.

Numerous ladies employed as petrol attendants over the years including three sisters; Violet, from 1970 until 1988 Dorothy, 1973 to 1977 and Pat, 1985 to 1989. Others were Mrs Muriel Early, 1971 to 1980, Terina Hooper, 1982 to 1987, Judith Morris 1990 to 1998 and Margaret May from1991 to1998.

Father at the new petrol pumps.

The mechanics employed for the first few years were Harry Dummer as foreman, Cyril Jones as fitter and Ernie Flashman, who serviced the cars (changing oils and filters and greasing all the steering and brake rod pivots).

In 1954 a new canopy was erected over the forecourt and new pumps were installed with financial help from the BP petrol company. As you can see in the photo above, Father is standing at the new petrol pumps.

During the same time, the smaller of the workshops, made of corrugated metal sheets over a steel frame, was demolished and a brick building with a flat roof erected in its place (which is still there). This building became the office, and tyre store with a small office attached for the petrol attendants.

When I became workshop manager I would have a cup of tea every morning and catch up with the latest gossip with the petrol attendants. Occasionally I would clean out the filters in the petrol pumps as the petrol had a lot of contamination in it (mainly rust) from the oil tankers and delivery lorries. The filter cleaning would be done by removing a plate from the side of the pump secured by three bolts, loosing about half a litre of fuel. The filter was then washed it in clean petrol and any rust in the bottom of the filter holder scooped out before re- assembly.

Around that time a company based in Cardiff (who shall remain nameless) bought a large number of petrol stations across South Wales and sold cheaper petrol. This was more contaminated than usual causing dozens of vehicles to break down when their fuel systems were blocked. They weren't in business long as the complaints mounted. It was rumoured that the petrol came from the dregs in the bottom of seagoing tankers based in Amsterdam. During the mid 1950s there was stock car racing in Neath Abbey to the west of the Abbey ruins, where the brake- down truck was used to tow the damaged cars off the track.

MAIN SHOWROOM

The showroom and the land up to the electricity sub-station on Sidings Terrace were purchased from Harold Fenn and his family in 1966. They specialised in American cars that had been left here after the war. Harold had a son called Harold junior and a grandson called young Harold. The latter at the time of writing still runs the garage his grandfather used in Grahams Terrace in Skewen.

The showroom was unfinished with no doors along the front or any decoration inside. We completed the building with heavy wooden sliding doors with glass panels (which are still there in good condition after 45 years). Over the years various small plots were bought on the western side of the showroom. These included the offices that were attached to the showroom then the Cresta filling station, and finally the body repair shop from Savage Motors which was converted into a showroom that held the Stadium Executive Cars, then later new Toyota and Kia cars.

CWMDU BRICKWORKS

To the east of Lucy Road stood the Cwmdu brickworks, which had been originally owned by John John who lived in Lon-Las Manor House (now demolished) above Park Drive. He owned all the area north of the Swansea to London railway line and from the brook next to the Bowens Arms to Dynevor Place. It is said that he was paid half a penny for every ton of bricks produced in Cwmdu brickworks until 1900 when an auction was held and most of the estate was sold off.

J Brooks Taylor bought an area that included Number 2 to Number 8 Lucy Road, the workshops and the brickworks at the auction. His name was on the brickworks chimney stack until its demolition in the 1960s.

In 1949 the brickworks, workshops and the quarry behind were bought by Evan Evans Bevan.

Between the workshops and the brickworks stood a single storey building, which was the brickworks office and living accommodation. On the right was the office while on the left and to the rear on the right, there were rooms that two families lived in; on the left Trevor Davies and his wife Vera lived where they brought up two sons. Howard, who became a fully qualified welder and Francis John, who went into hairdressing and has two premises in Skewen and Swansea called F. Js.

In the right rear of the building lived a collier who built a shed in which he put a coal-fired boiler and a bath. He would let Trevor's boys use the bath on Sundays as a special treat.

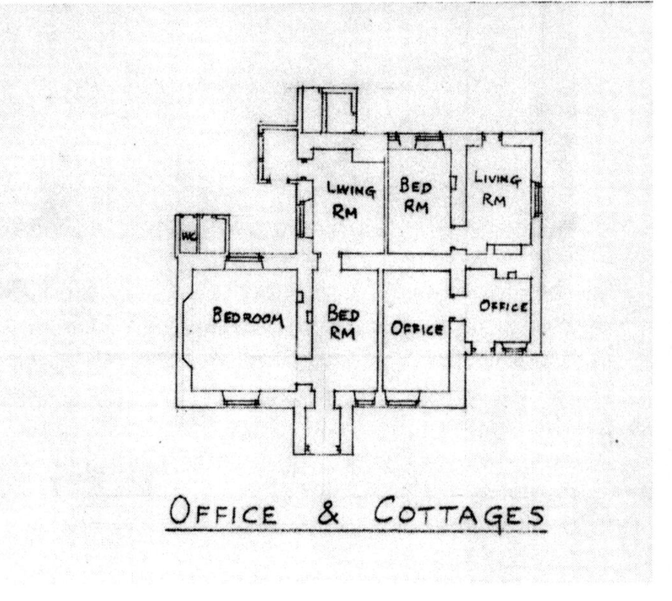

There was another small building near to the brick kiln in which the night watchman would be located and was a regular stop for the local policeman on night patrol to have a cup of tea.

During the following years the quarry was cut in a westerly direction behind Lucy Road, eventually incorporating a small drift mine, which had, during the 1940s—50s yielded fifteen tons of coal per week, worked by one man with a horse and cart which he delivered to Bill Hickman, a coal merchant on the High Street in Skewen. The mine was also used as an air raid shelter during WW2.

In 1942 a bomb dropped on Sidings Terrace in the middle of the road outside Number 4 which started a fire in a paint store across the road that became huge with paint tins exploding in the heat (the local children thought it was gunfire). A number of the very large storage tanks at the Llandarcy refinery were also set ablaze that night.

During the war the local Civil Defence Corps used the brickworks and the kilns as exercise areas, using Stirrup pumps whose intake was placed in a bucket of water and pumped vigorously to extinguish small fires and they would parade up and down Lucy Road with wooden rifles until proper ones were available.

ANDERSON SHELTERS

Anderson shelters (named after the Home Secretary at that time) made of metal sheets were supplied to anyone who applied for them. The first was issued in February 1939 to householders in Islington London. 2,250 were issued nationwide during the war. Households earning less than £250 per year would get one free, while those earning more had to pay either in cash or what they called then delayed payment (hire purchase) with 37% interest! They were made of steel sheets about ten feet long and curved at one end to form the roof when bolted together. After digging a large hole in a suitable place (usually at the bottom of the garden away from the house), the shelter was then assembled and placed in the hole and covered by earth in which vegetables were grown.

Anderson shelter

WORLD WAR 2

After the outbreak of war in September 1939 a number of laws and regulations were introduced. Among them was one that decreed all gold coins had to be taken to a bank and sold to the Treasury. All theatres and cinemas were closed but reopened shortly afterwards to keep up morale. Everyone had to carry a gas mask with them at all times.

Later that month petrol rationing was imposed; every vehicle owner had to collect a book of coupons proving ownership by showing their registration book. The allocation of petrol per week was dependent on the occupation of the owner.

As the German bombing raids became heaver there came an urgent need for fire engines, so a large number of pre-war Austin Twelve cars were converted by having the rear end made into a canvas-covered seating for four fire-fighters and a tow bar fitted to haul the fire pump. Later Austin lorries became available with built-in fire pumps some of which still exist today and are called "Green Goddesses".

Food was also rationed with every household given a number of ration books depending on the number living there and each book had to be registered with the appropriate shop (butcher, baker, fishmonger and grocer etc.) each shopkeeper had to keep a list of their registered customers and only serve them as they were only allocated enough produce to cover their list. Rationing ended slowly over a number of years with various foods coming off until 1950.

Two small aircraft crashed in the Skewen area during those years, the first was an RAF Boulton-Paul Defiant fighter with a crew of two; a pilot and a radio operator/gunner in a turret behind the pilot with 4 Vickers machine guns.

They had been very effective above the beaches of Dunkirk shooting down 65 enemy aircraft during the evacuation. The German pilots, thinking they were Hurricanes or Spitfires, attacked from above and behind into the sights of the machine guns.

Boulton-Paul Defiant fighter

The one that came down here was near Len Potter's house at the west end of Lucy Road. It was based at Pembrey airfield to the west of Llanelli. It's rumoured that one night in the Officers mess there was a discussion about the effectiveness of the barrage balloons that were flown near important areas.

Barrage balloon

The next day, two of the New Zealand airmen based there decided to find out how effective they were and unfortunately found that they were very effective when they collided with the cable of a balloon anchored near the Star public house in Llansamlet. After hitting the cable the turret was detached by the gunner and the guns started firing, (luckily no one on the ground was hurt). It landed on a building below Len's house, which was then Tom Walter's workshop before he moved to Evelyn Road. I'm told that the mechanics put some live bullets in a vice and hit them with a hammer to fire them!

Both the crew got out, but were too low for their parachutes to open properly. One was found in a tree and pronounced dead. The other landed in a field, which is now covered by Park Crescent, and died later in the day.

The second air crash was near Drummau Hall. When an RAF trainer came down in thick fog and both occupants were killed.

THE BEVIN BOYS

During the first years of WW2 there were so many coal mining strikes that almost half the working days were lost. The main cause was the discontentment that still festered in the work force since the 1926 strike. Their wages were in the eightieth place of the 100 important industries in the war effort, when women were recruited to the factories and were paid a lot more: sometimes three times as much. Also, so many men volunteered to go into the armed forces that production was badly affected leaving only the older men, so all ex-miners were drafted in to help, but this was not successful as there were still not enough men to produce the increased amount required, and the old machinery was beginning to wear out.

Drastic measures were called for, so the Minister of Labour, Ernest Bevin, returned thirty thousand men who had mining experience from the forces, but again that was not enough to supply the coal needed. Next he introduced a system in late 1943 which stated that for every man eligible to be called up into the forces, one in ten was chosen by ballot to work in the coal industry. This was when the name Bevin Boys was first used. These men came from all kinds of jobs - some from offices or banks and other light duties with no experience of manual work. They found that working in the dark with picks and shovels very hard and with blisters forming on their hands and knees. Some mines had pithead baths but the unlucky ones had to walk home or to lodgings in their working clothes before having a bath. Very often they would call at the local pub to quench their thirst and that's where a number of male voice choirs were formed. The singing would get rid of some of the coal dust in their lungs.

These men did not have any official recognition until the late twentieth century as they had kept secret their wartime work; being afraid to be called conscientious objectors; people who would not fight in any war as a matter of conscience.

LUCY ROAD WORKSHOP

This building was erected in the 1920s, when the Richmond Bus Company used it until December 1950 when they amalgamated with a number of other companies to form The United Welsh Bus Company.

Stadium Transport rented these premises from Evan Evans Bevan in 1952 for £8 a week as workshops and then sublet a third of it to the Llandarcy oil refinery for £3 per week to store a special powder for use in the refining process.

In 1958 it was purchased by Stadium Transport and also the yard behind it. A large wooden building was erected in the yard which became Stadium Transport's main office. It had been a scout hut at Pengam in the Rhymney Valley. Brian Jones remembers going up there to dismantle it and then reassembling in the yard. On a wall in the office there was a large map with circles drawn on it centred on Skewen showing the distances the A, B and C, licences could be used (see page 89) and also the cost of haulage for those distances. The building was used as the company office for a number of years until a two-storey office block was built on to the side of the workshop.

Another feature near the workshop was a brook that ran from the quarry alongside Number 8 Lucy Road over the unmade road and down to the main road between Numbers 9 and 10 Sidings Terrace. Early in the twentieth century this source of water was used by the steam engines and steam rollers to refill their tanks - twenty gallons each - when doing road repairs in the area. It was also used by A. Richards Haulage Contractors of Newport as an overnight stop for their steam Lorries when travelling across south

Wales. The stream dried up eventually as quarrying progressed across the hill.

Steam engine *Steam roller*

The floor of the workshops when it was bought had two inches of hardened grease covering it. After weeks of work, with very large blow lamps on wheels we melted the grease and scraped it away a millimetre at a time. The floor was later surfaced with terrazzo tiles which were still in good condition when the building was demolished in 2009.

Halfway along the front of the building was a large sliding door, big enough for the double-decker buses to enter when it was used by the Richmond Bus Company. To the right of this door two hinged doors were fitted as access to the section the oil works had rented. This later became the tyre fitting depot for Stadium Transport's lorries, where Billy Richards and his son worked. The main part of the building was used to repair cars for Stadium Garage car sales and their customers.

We overhauled engines for our customers, having removed the engines and stripped them down. The cylinder blocks and crankshafts were sent to Swansea auto services, based at Meadow Street off Gors Avenue. in Swansea. (est. 1946). The cylinder heads on the overhead valve engines were reconditioned by us. This included making sure the surfaces of the exhaust and inlet valves were perfectly matched to their seating. This was done by using a special grinding paste (Carborundum) which is still in use today. It was contained in a small cylindrical tin with a lid on either end, coarse paste at one end and fine on the other. Coarse was used first then fine to finish off. It would be smeared on the contact surface of the valves and a sucker on a wooden stick was used to spin the valve to and fro between the palms of the hands on its seating until both surfaces had a smooth light grey finish.

Valve grinding equipment

An important health precaution we took was to apply a barrier cream to our hands before starting a job and reapplying it every time we washed them. The soap we used was a semi-liquid type, usually Swarfega, which was very effective to keep our hands dermatitis-free and under the fingernails clean. The young ladies were very appreciative of this as clean fingernails and polished shoes were required to attract their attention in those days. As the Fairy Liquid TV advert said: "The hands that clean dishes can be soft as your face."

When cars of this era were new or the engine had been reconditioned the cylinder head bolts had to be tightened down to the manufactures specification, the engine oil changed after the first 300 miles and every 3,000 miles thereafter. At 12,000miles it was drained and filled with flushing oil. The engine was then run for three minutes at low speed, drained and refilled with the proper grade of oil.

Also when new or if the engine had been reconditioned, it was advised to drive steadily for first few hundred miles at no more than 15mph in first gear, 25mph in second, 40mph in third and 50 mph in fourth. A 'RUNNING IN PLEASE PASS' sign was displayed in the rear window.

After the first service (300 miles) it was advised to increase the speed steadily to prolong the life of the engine. Daily checks were engine oil and water levels and a visual tyre pressure check (usually a kick of each tyre would do). Weekly checks included the battery acid level.

It was recommended that lighter oil (SAE 30) was used in the winter and heavier (SAE 40) in the summer: multi-grade oils had not been developed then. The SAE stands for Society of Automotive Engineers who graded the oil into various thicknesses ranging from SAE 10 for small delicate machinery to SAE100 for large slow moving appliances.

Another chore(before antifreeze came available) was draining the cooling system every night during the winter months through drain taps at the bottom of the radiator and on the side of the engine then refilling with warm water the following morning. When antifreeze was first introduced it was mixed with water at a ratio of 25/1, one quarter of the capacity of the cooling system for the winter months. In the Spring the mixture was drained out and the system filled with clean water until the following autumn. The engine would overheat during the summer if the mixture was left in. Today the mixture put in during manufacture has a different chemical formula and can be left in for a number of years.

An oil heater could be placed under the engine during the colder winter nights to keep the oil warm, so that the engine would be easer to start, especially when using a starting handle.

These pre-war and early post-war cars and small vans had numerous greasing points on the brake rod pivots (hydraulic brakes came later) and steering joints which had to be lubricated every 1,000 miles using a grease gun copper mesh fuel pump filter had to be cleaned and gearbox and rear axle oil levels checked. Every 5000miles all the oils were changed and the front wheel bearings removed, washed thoroughly and repacked with special grease.

Grease gun

Father used to play a trick on us; he would touch a spark plug on an engine that was running and grab someone nearby by the hand, giving them a shock. He could also stop an engine by putting his hands on all four sparkplugs, at that time the power to the sparkplugs was significantly lower than today.

Some of the tricks we played on the apprentices whilst working on the hearses we had in frequently for repair was that someone would hide in the compartment below where the coffin is carried and a black curtain was draped over the opening. The boy was asked to stand behind to see if the rear lights worked. As he stood there a hand would appear from beneath the curtain and grab his leg which made him jump and shout giving everyone else a good laugh. Another was to send him down to the village ironmongers for a left handed spanner or sky hook.

One of the dirtiest jobs we did in those days was to under-seal the new cars. This entailed wearing special clothing and a mask when spraying the underside of the car with a dark brown sealant to prevent rusting as the technique of dipping the car bodies in a sealant before painting at the factory had yet to be introduced.

I remember a local skin and hide company, (which transported cow hides from slaughter houses to tanneries to be made into leather), purchased two new Ford lorries from us that needed three differently-coloured coats of a special sealant sprayed over the chassis and the wooden body. The first coat was yellow, the second red and the final one blue. When I went home in the evening my family knew by the spots on my glasses which colour I'd used that day. Another disliked job was to de-grease every new car. This grease had been applied to the paintwork at the factory to prevent any dust or industrial fallout damaging it during storage and delivery.

There were a number of vehicles that we disliked working on. One was a Ford Cortina belonging to a farmer from the top of the Neath valley who carried calves in the boot that got excited and fouled the inside including the wiring and bulb holders of the rear lights, which had to be cleaned to get them to work again. Another was a butcher's little black and white van that always had bones in the engine compartment which had been carried in there overnight by rats while the engine was warm. None of our staff bought meat from that shop. The scariest of all was a time when the bonnet was opened on a Ford Zephyr and a dead cat was found jammed between the top of the radiator and the bonnet. It had been there a long time as it was dried out and mummified.

THE M.O.T. TEST

The Ministry of Transport annual test was first introduced in the U.K. in 1960 by Mr Ernest Marples for cars and light vans over 10 years old as there was concern about the safety of these vehicles. Mr Marples' famous saying was "When driving, always expect the unexpected." The early tests were for steering, lights and brakes only, but gradually over the years more items have been added and the age brought down to over three yrs old. At the time of writing, it now includes exhaust emissions for both diesel and petrol engines and numerous other items.

To become an official testing station, permission has to be sought from the Ministry of Transport who would inspect the premises for suitable access, adequate parking and a number of other conditions before the purchase of the specialist equipment needed.

In 1960 this equipment included a brake-tester (decellarometer) which was placed on the front passenger side floor and the vehicle driven at 20mph along a safe road and the footbrake applied. The reading on the machine was then noted, and this was repeated for the handbrake. The stopping distance guidelines recommended were 27ft for the footbrake and 54ft for the handbrake for vehicles with four wheel brakes, 2 wheeled brakes 45ft. 3-wheelers and motorcycles 45ft.

Some years later V. L. Churchill introduced a machine they called a brake efficiency recorder. This was larger and quite heavy. It had a pendulum arm with a ballpoint tip that would swing forward when the brakes were applied to mark a line on a card that was placed on its curved surface. On the top of the pendulum there was a spirit level which had to be centralised so that the pen would run along the card to show the brake efficiency. This was very hard to set when testing on an undulating road like Lucy Road. The vehicle would be driven to the spot were the test was to be carried out and the machine which had been placed on the floor on the front left-hand side was centralised using the spirit level. It was then reversed back far enough for it to be travelling at 20mph at the test spot, and the whole process repeated for the handbrake, if the ballpoint pen worked, which it frequently didn't.

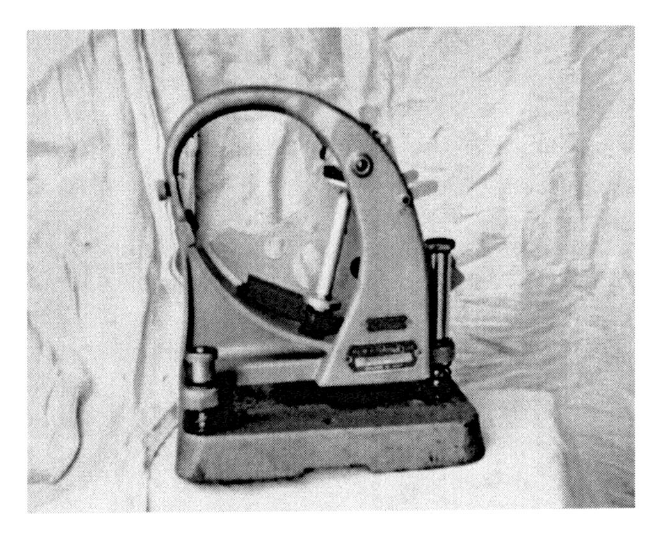

Churchill brake tester

These machines had to be sent to the manufacturer every two years to be calibrated, and a certificate issued was kept safe for the ministry inspectors to check when they came to inspect all the necessary equipment needed to perform the tests

Test Certificate

CHURCHILL
999
BRAKE EFFICIENCY
RECORDER

This instrument has been tested on apparatus and by a method approved by the National Physical Laboratory with the following results:

RECORDER SERIAL NO. 2284

Maximum Value of Mean Deceleration for minimum period of 0·2 seconds	Instrument Reading
69	71
54	52
30	30

Date 4th June 1970.

Inspector's Signature

Note: This certificate guarantees the accuracy of the instrument at the above date. Please follow instructions closely when using instrument.

V. L. CHURCHILL & Co. Ltd.,
LONDON ROAD, DAVENTRY,
NORTHANTS, ENGLAND

VLC/213/10/65

When the rolling road brake testers were introduced they consisted of a pair of rollers driven by electric motors set in the workshop floor, where the front wheels and then the rear (including handbrake) are tested separately. They are still in use today but linked to a computer that prints out the results.

PWLL BACH COLLIERY

The mine had originally opened in 1812, when anthracite was extracted from the 'Red Vein' which runs across south

Wales and is thirty-six inches (92 cms) high in this area. It closed down a few years later but was reopened in 1886 by David William Davies (Davies Aberlash) who, after many setbacks, made it a profitable concern. In 1911 he formed the Pwllbach Colliery Company employing 120 men. In 1913 the first tunnel was cut from the mine to the other side of the Gwrhyd Mountain. When a new seam was found in 1922 a second tunnel was cut out to the Swansea Valley, emerging near the roundabout to the south side of Ystalyfera, where the coal was loaded into trucks and taken down to Swansea docks on a branch line of the London Midland and Scottish railway .Mrs. Meredith, a farmer's wife living on the Gwrhyd Mountain, would take advantage of this tunnel and walk through it to Ystalyfera to play Bingo.

SOUTH WALES COAL MINES

In 1911 nearly four million tons of anthracite was produced in South Wales, (92% of the total UK production of this type of coal). It was sent all over the world to refuel the ships as they travelled from port to port. This process was called "bunkering."

At the colliery surface the coal was washed then poured onto a sloping surface which had a series of holes; smaller ones near the top so as the coal slid down the smaller lumps would fall through first and as the holes got bigger the larger ones would fall. The largest size was called Cobbles and others in decreasing sizes were called Nuts (German, Paris and French). Peanuts, Beans, Peas, Grains, Rubbly Culm and Duff. The latter was the very small grains and dust and was made into cobbles by mixing it with clay in a plant at the colliery. I remember making them on the farm (they were about three inches (8cms) in diameter) for use in our fires.

There were hundreds of small drifts mines all over south Wales with ingenious methods of working them. In the lower Swansea Valley the drams were hauled from underground by using the rear axle of an old lorry whose front end had been embedded in concrete. The cable that was attached to the drams was wound around one of the rear wheels and the engine of the lorry was started up and an appropriate gear selected depending on the weight to be hauled up. At one near Crymlyn Farm in Skewen they used an old Bedford lorry engine to drive a ventilation fan (which I repaired a number of times).

COLLIERY TRAMWAYS

1826 saw one of the earliest tramways built in south Wales by John Parsons running from the Primrose colliery just outside Rhos down Primrose Lane and through Alltwen to a private wharf on the Swansea canal at Pontardawe. The rails were only 24 inches apart and the drams were moved by horses on the gentler slopes while steam powered winches were used on the steepest gradients Other tramways used a method where the full drams at the top to be let down the slope were linked to the empty ones at the bottom, the weight of the full ones going down would pull the empty ones up. In some instances a water tank was attached to the full drams for extra weight and was emptied at the bottom.

COAL MINING SAFETY PRECAUSIONS

One of the many safety features of the coal mining industry was the use of metal discs (tags) about an inch (two and a half centimetres) in diameter with each miner's personal number stamped on it. Before being carried down on a spacke (a number of drams modified to carry people up and down the incline) or being lowered down the pit shaft in a cage (up to several hundred feet), they would hand in their disc at the lamp room and in exchange would receive their lamp. In the pits where the gas level was high every seventh miner would also have a Davy lamp. At the end of the shift the lamps were handed back in and the disc returned to them so the lamp room staff could account for each miner. In the early days they had a naked flame lit by carbide powder. During the 1930s battery-powered lamps were introduced. These were clamped onto the helmet with a cable running down to a battery clipped onto the waist belt.

The first to have the new type lamps were the senior men who could then be spotted coming along the roadways because the light would move from side to side as they walked warning the others that they were near.

THE DAVY LAMP

The Davy lamp was created by Sir Humphrey Davy in 1815. It was a safety lamp for use in coal mines where there was a likelihood of flammable gas in the air under ground. The original lamp used heavy vegetable oil as fuel, and a canvas strip an inch wide was placed vertically in the oil which soaked it up and the top end set alight to illuminate the dark passages. Its main purpose was to detect gas, (methane and other gasses called firedamp or mine damp). The inventor found that if the flame was placed inside a certain size wire mesh it would change colour but would not cause an explosion. This lamp increased the safety factor enormously so that deeper coal seams could be worked.

The accident rate was reduced dramatically with new equipment and regulations introduced. The explosions which frequently occurred were caused by the mixture of methane gas which is a by-product of centuries of rotting vegetation and is lighter than air so it collects at the roof of the tunnels and when mixed with oxygen becomes a lethal concoction which explodes if a flame or spark comes near it. This happened regularly in the early days when the miners used carbide lamps which had a naked flame. During that time a method of detecting the gas was to carry a canary in a cage that was held up near the roof as they walked along. When it fell off its perch they would know there was gas there. When the cage was lowered the bird would recover. That practice was abandoned when the Davy lamp was invented.

One little known precaution was the use of very fine stone dust to cover the floor and ledges of the airway tunnels (up to two inches deep) to keep down the coal dust that floated in the air, also overhead platforms were built and mounds of stone dust pilled up there so if an explosion did occur this dust would be blown along the airways and stop the flames from spreading.

To ventilate the mines a shaft was cut to the surface (the one for Pwllbach was horizontal and came out next to a pub in Ystalyfera) where a furnace with a tall chimney was built so that the action of the fire when lit would draw out the foul air. In various parts of the roadways fireproof sheets about four feet wide made of canvas coated with tar, later plastic (called bradishes), were hung to direct the air flow to the correct locations.

On reaching the bottom of the shaft in some pits they had to walk a mile or more to the coal face to start their shift unless they were lucky when an empty line of drams was going their way. Each shift would be calculated from the time they went underground to the time they were back at the bottom ready to be transported to the surface, so that meant in some mines two hours of the seven-hour shift were spent getting to and from the coalface. In some mines where there was a steep incline on the way to the face a moving track was suspended from the roof with ropes hanging down for the men to hold onto to ascend (hanging straps). In the latter years when the coalface was up to two miles from the bottom of the shaft or incline, man-riding cars often called “Paddy mails” were used so that the men were still fresh to do a longer stint at the coalface. In some pits the morning shift production was so high that the winding gear to the surface could not cope, so the excess coal would be stored in large room-sized hoppers (known as bunkers) that were emptied during the afternoon shift

The height of the coal seam varied considerably in different parts of the coalfield and from pit to pit; sometimes as low as eighteen inches (45cms). In the lower seam pits the hewers (as they were called) would lay on their side to dig out the coal, passing it back by hand to a younger man or an apprentice who would scoop it into a basket made of the same material as the bradishes (canvas soaked in tar) and drag it along to the dram in the very dim light reflected back off the coal face from the hewer's lamp. In some places the men had to push the dram along the rails

to where the there was enough height for a horse to be used. The horse would then pull it to the bottom of the pit shaft in deep mines or to the bottom of the incline in drift mines.

In the pits the drams were loaded into a cage to be lifted to the surface while in the drift mines they were attached to a cable and pulled up to the surface by a steam-powered winch in the early days and electric motors later.

In some pits electricity was generated in turbine houses built near the top on the surface. The drams were then moved on the underground roadways using electric locomotives. When new machines for cutting the coal were installed they too were electrically driven, as were the conveyer belts that took the coal from the cutting machine to the bottom of the pit or to the surface if it was an incline. There were also man-belts on which the colliers would lay and be taken to and from the working area instead of walking miles each day.

When air tools (pneumatic picks and drills) were introduced to the coal face, buildings were erected near the top of the pit shaft or incline to house a large air compressor which supplied high pressure air to power the tools. The pipe carrying this air would run down and along underground roadway, sometimes for two or three miles or more, and still have enough pressure to drive the tools and the compressed air haulage engines. They used progressively smaller diameter pipes to keep the pressure high enough.

There was another group of men working below ground called the packers; their job was to fill in the spaces from where the coal had been extracted with slabs of rock to prevent the roof from falling onto the roadways, while in other areas called the “gob” or "goaf ", the roof was allowed to fall.

Most miners would chew chewing tobacco called plover or twist and spat out a mixture of coal dust and spittle, and would also cough up the coal dust from their lungs for the rest of their lives as Father often did, exclaiming “get out and walk.”

A trick they would use on an apprentice was cut a small lump of rubber off a conveyor belt rub it in the tobacco in their pouch and hand it to the boy to chew. Some would arrive next day saying how good it was and it lasted so long. Another was to tell the boy that the wooden pit prop was too short and would ask him to pull at one end to stretch it. One of their favourite sayings was “keep a cool head and a sharp mandrill” (a pick for cutting out the coal).

PIT PONIES

This was the name given to the type of horse that worked underground in the coalmines because of their small sturdy size to cope with the cramped conditions in the tunnels and stables underground. They were worked down there for eleven and a half months every year, only brought up during what was called 'stop fortnight' which was the last week in July and the first week in August when all the mines closed for their annual holidays. For the first few days they were kept in darkened stables so that their eyes could gradually get used to the sunlight. They obviously relished this short break as they would run around the fields swishing their tails (which were tied up for the rest of the year) and thoroughly enjoying themselves. When it came to take them back down, the hauliers had great difficulty in capturing them. In the drift mines (sloping tunnels) the horses were led down to the stables: in some pits they were stood on their hind legs in the cage, whilst in others the cage was lifted higher than normal and the horses strapped in slings under the cage. Some horses struggled so violently that they broke loose and fell to their deaths down the pit shaft.

They were sometimes supplied by a local farmer who had a contract with the mine owner. One such arrangement was between Mr Charles Henry Paterson of Trenache Farm, Bryncoch near Neath and Charles Evan Thomas, proprietor of the Gnoll Colliery, Neath.

the contract read as follows, *This agreement made the 29th day of September 1883 between Charles Evan Thomas proprietor of The Gnoll Colliery Neath in the County of Glamorgan by Thomas Jones Price his lawful authorized agent of the one part and Charles Henry Patterson of Trenache farm near Neath aforesaid farmer of the other part as follows:*

1 The said Charles Henry Paterson let on hire and the aforesaid proprietor will take on hire Five Horses for working for the most part underground at the said colliery from the seventh day of October 1883.

2 The said proprietor will pay the said farmer for the use on hire of the five horses working as afore said the sum of Eight Shillings per week for each horse.

The said several weekly sums shall be paid monthly on the monthly pay days at the said colliery.

3 The horses shall be stabled fed and shod and receive the usual farriers attention bestowed upon horses at collieries at the cost of the said proprietor.

4 The farmer shall provide collars for each of the said horses, such collars to be kept in repair by the said proprietor who will at the expiration or termination of this contract return the same in good repair, ordinary wear and tear only excepted

5 The horses shall be worked by the said proprietor but he shall not in any way be liable for loss of or damage to the said horses or any of them by death or sickness or accident howsoever occasioned, any such loss shall be borne by the said farmer and he shall from time to time forthwith on demand provide or replace other good horses in the place or instead of those which shall have died or become unable or unfit for effective work.

6 Subject to any sale or purchase of the said horses or any of them as hereinafter provided the said hiring of the said horses shall be from the said seventh day of October 1883 for twenty four weeks certain and onwards until either party give to the other eight weeks notice to terminate the hiring.

7 The said proprietor shall have the option of purchasing all or anyone or more of the said horses at any time before the 1st of December 1883 on giving notice thereof to the said farmer, such purchase to be of the price which such horse or horses would be likely to fetch in the market and such price in case of difference is to be ascertained and determined by reference to arbitration in the usual way. In case the said proprietor shall exercise his said option of purchase this agreement so far as regards the horse or horses which he shall elect to purchase and determine as and from the completion of such purchase but in other respect shall continue. The said farmer shall be paid at the sale aforesaid for the hire or use of such one or more of the said horses as shall be purchased as aforesaid up to the completion of such purchase and any part of the week shall be duly apportioned.'

THE FIRST BRITISH COAL MINE?

One of the first recorded coal mines in the U.K. was owned by Sir George Bruce of Carnock from Culross in Fife, Scotland. He started it in 1575 well before the Industrial Revolution and it was the first coal mine in the world to go out under the sea. About a quarter of a mile off shore he built a large brick circular hollow structure. Its purpose was to ventilate the coal mine by using the warm air rising from the mine through the shaft drawing fresh air along the underground roadway from the shore.

It was considered one of the marvels of the British Isles in the 17th century for the ingenious methods used to drain out the constant water (probably using a windmill) as well as the ventilation system. It was destroyed during a huge storm in 1625.

The first steam powered water pump was used in the west country by the inventor Thomas Newcamden in 1712.

BRITISH SPANNER AND BOLT SIZES

The first standard size nuts, bolts and spanners in the world were proposed by British engineer Joseph Whitworth in 1841 when he addressed the British Standards Institution in London where his idea was adopted. Up to this time every industry had its own sizes. His system had the spanner size marked with the diameter of the bolts starting from 1/8 inch up to 2inch and was called BSW (British Standard Whitworth).

In 1884 the BA (British Association) sizes were formulated then standardised in 1903, and were later used instead of BSW for all sizes below ¼ inch.

In 1908 BSF British Standard Fine was introduced, this not only had a finer thread but a smaller bolt head and nut (one size down from BSW); therefore no change of spanner sizes was required.

During 1948 it was decided to drop the BSW and BSF sizes in favour of the A/F size (across flat) which was the distance across the head of the bolt. This had been used in the USA for sometime, and did mean another set of spanners. The 1970s saw the introduction of metric sizes. This meant three sets of spanners and sockets had to be kept in the toolboxes of anyone working in engineering for a number of years.

TOLL AND TURNPIKE ROADS

Up until the late 1600s the roads in Britain had been repaired by the Parish Councils. There were some good lengths and others very badly maintained depending on the wealth of the Council.

Around 1700 turnpike roads and toll bridges came into being when the users had to pay to pass over them. They were maintained by either a local group of businessmen or the squire of the area. The fee depended on what they were carrying in their carts or animals they were driving. Toll houses were built at the end of a length of road or at a bridge and a barrier placed across the road where an employee would collect the money.

A TYPICAL TOLLHOUSE.

By 1750 there were 5,000 miles of toll roads in the U.K. and by 1770 there had been a large increase to 25,000 miles. Long lengths were by then controlled by turnpike trusts and tar macadam had been invented, cutting down journey times by hours and sometimes days. For example, the time from Edinburgh to London came down from thirteen days to three days at an average speed of fifteen miles per hour with overnight stops at coaching inns.

The tenant farmers in west Wales got very annoyed because some of the roads in their area were still in a very poor state of repair as the money collected was not used for maintaining the roads but other projects. Their carts would frequently be damaged when driving along these badly rutted and potholed roads. They formed themselves into gangs dressed as women calling themselves the daughters of Rebecca and attacked the tollhouses, destroying a number of them between 1839 and 1843; one at Pontardulais and another in Hendy. In Pontardulais there is a stone erected to commemorate these attacks located about two hundred yards up the hill from the Fountain Inn on the Pontlliw road. A toll house in Neath, undamaged during the riots, was situated at the bottom of Cimla Road. where the Territorial army buildings are now situated. The last toll was paid there in 1884.

ROAD TRANSPORT

1905 saw the Automobile Association formed which, after royal patronage, became the Royal Automobile Club (RAC). Also in 1905 the first "filling station" was opened by Sylvanus F. Bowser in Indiana U.S.A. whose surname became a name for mobile fuel supply vehicles in the military and for refuelling machines on building sites. A year later the first RAC patrols were on the roads on bicycles, mainly to warn their members of police speed traps. In 1911 the American carmaker, Cadillac, fitted the first starter motor. 1914 saw the introduction of petrol pumps at the roadside in the UK as up to then only two-gallon cans had been available. Five years later (1919) the first traffic lights were installed in America and the following year the first hydraulic brakes were fitted to cars in America.

In 1923 the first roundabout was introduced in the UK but the priority rule was not enforced until 1966, that is to give way to traffic coming from your right when entering the roundabout. Things were quiet until 1930 when the 20mph speed limit was abolished. Cars carrying less than seven people had no limit at all. The minimum driving age was also set at seventeen and compulsory third-party insurance (this covered other people's vehicles and property only) had to be bought. During the rest of the 1930s the first Highway Code was published priced one penny. Cats' eyes were used from 1934, (these are placed at intervals along the white lines between each carriageway). The compulsory driving test, provisional driving licences and "L" plates were introduced in 1935. Two years later dipping headlights, speedometers and safety glass windscreens were made compulsory on new vehicles.

At the outbreak of the second world war (1939) petrol rationing was introduced and driving tests suspended, all street lights switched off, a 20mph speed limit after dark to save accidents as all vehicles had to be fitted with a headlight hood which had a slit across it half an inch high with a hood above so that no light would shine upward for the enemy aircraft to follow the roads to find their targets. British Summer time was also introduced (the clocks are still turned back one hour during the winter) as a precaution to minimise pedestrian road casualties with the extra hour of daylight in the evenings. After the war (1946), driving tests were resumed but had a period of one year for anyone with a wartime provisional driving license to have a full licence without taking the test.

In 1950 the first safety belts were used in the USA to stop sleeping passengers from falling out of the cars. In the same year petrol rationing ended in the UK.

Radial-ply tyres came on the market in 1953 and a year later flashing indicator lights had to be fitted to all new vehicles and ones up to two years old.

During the Suez crisis in 1955 petrol was again rationed and learner drivers could drive without a qualified passenger (to save fuel) and driving tests were again suspended. 1958 saw the introduction of the dreaded parking meter while two years later meter maids (traffic wardens) came onto the London streets and MOT tests started. The first self-service petrol pumps appeared in 1961 but the petrol attendants had to help as most motorists couldn't use them or didn't want the smell of petrol or diesel on their hands.

1965 saw the introduction of a temporary 70 mph speed limit on motorways, 60 mph on dual carriageways with central reservation barriers and 50 mph if no barriers and some bypasses, 30 mph on most other roads except by today near schools and certain housing estates were it's 20 mph. In the same year rear brake warning lights had to be fitted to all new vehicles.

The infamous drink-drive law was enforced in 1967 and the fitting of front seatbelts made compulsory, also MOT tests brought down to three years old or over and tyre condition added to the test.

Reflective number plates were made compulsory in 1973. Six years later rear fog lamps had to be fitted to new cars and in 1983 the wearing of front safety belts was made compulsory. From 1987 rear seat belts were fitted on new cars. A year later all new cars had to have engines that could use unleaded petrol.

The following year (1992) the fitting of catalytic converters to the exhaust systems on new cars was enforced to cut down the noxious exhaust fumes).

BRITISH VEHICLE TAXATION

Road tax was first paid by horse-drawn Hackney carriages (forerunner of the taxi) in London in 1637 because their number had grown so high that traffic jams were a regular problem. A hundred years later it was extended to all carriages drawn by two or more horses and in 1770 included steam powered vehicles.

In the Locomotive Acts of 1861-65 a speed limit of four miles per hour on open roads and two miles per hour in towns and villages was imposed with a man waving a red flag walking in front of each vehicle. A road tax of £2/2- per year on every self propelled Vehicle was also imposed.

In 1919-20 legislation was passed to ensure that all self-propelled vehicles were taxed at a rate of £1 per horse power (work a horse could do in one hour) per year, and had to have a visible means of showing this in the form of a two-inch (6 cms) paper disc displayed on the front in a specially designed holder recommended by the Ministry of

Transport. In addition, each vehicle was issued with a registration number and log book.

Up until 1974 County Council offices were responsible for issuing the tax discs. During the early years they could only be used within the issuing county. This could be very expensive for anyone living near the border of a county and wanting to use it in the next, as they would have to purchase one for that county too. This all changed when the DVLA (Driver and Vehicle Licensing Authority) was formed with each county having its own registration letters.

Across South Wales we had DE for Pembrokeshire, for example ADE 123 then later 123 ADE up until 1963 when a letter was put before the numbers - A 123 ADE for 1963 and the next letter in the alphabet was used for each following year i.e. B for 1964 and so on.

Carmarthenshire was TH and BX,
Swansea CY and WN
Cardiff KG, BO and UH
Merthyr HB
Newport DW
Monmouthshire AX and WO
Glamorganshire NY, TG and TX

September 2001 saw further changes when the UK was divided into larger areas with their first letters. The prefix for Wales is C, Cardiff has CA to CO, Swansea has CP to CV and Bangor has CW and CX.

The numbers changes every May and September e.g. for Swansea CA 51 DBJ was from September 2001 to May1st 2002 then CA 02 DBJ to September 1st 2002 when it changed to 52 until May 2003 and so on until 2010 then CA 10 DBJ from May 1st until September 1st and CA 60 DBJ for the next 6 months.

GOODS VEHICLE LICENCES

In 1933 various goods vehicle licences were introduced. They consisted of type A to cover any load to any where in the U.K; type B to hire out the vehicle to carry other company's goods and type C to carry the owners own loads only. These were all abolished later on. When road transport was nationalised and the British Road Services formed, types A B C where replaced by type O which was a general licence covering all goods and distances. In addition, all vehicles weighing over 3.5 tonnes gross weight had to have a maintenance agreement with an approved garage. The exemptions were all vehicles used by the ambulance service, police, fire service and by the local authority for snow clearing or distribution of road salt. The circles on the map in Stadium Transports office indicated the distances from the office starting at up to five miles and then every five miles up to 35 miles so that the cost of the haulage could be calculated.

THE HISTORY OF TRANSPORT AND TRAVEL

The first form of transport by early humans around 7000 years ago was probably by sledge sliding over ice fields and the coarse grass of the plains. They may have had dogs and later cattle (they found that castrated bulls known as bullocks became docile and powerful) to do this work).

These bullocks (oxen) are still used today for this job in various parts of the world nowadays, pulling carts and ploughing fields.

There was discovered near Zurich in Switzerland one of the earliest wheeled vehicles dating from around 3000BC. At around this time they became an exclusive form of transport for the royalty and were thought so valuable that they were buried with the kings along with the oxen so they could be used in the afterlife.

By 2000 B.C. heavy wagons were in use across Europe and into the near east (Persia and Mesopotamia).During this time the chariot and the spoked wheel was invented. Up until then the wheels had been made from a solid peace of wood or from a number of planks tied together and shaped into a circle. The new wheel was much lighter and could absorb some of the shocks from the rough roads of that time.

The chariot became very popular with the nobility and kings; they were made of light wood with very delicate wheels. An example was found in Tutankhamen's tomb where the wheels were stored separately as the weight of the chariot would have damaged them if they had been left attached.

Up until the late 16th century the roads in Europe were rutted tracks with large potholes so only goods were transported along them: the able bodied rode on horseback and the infirm carried on litters drawn by horses.

Horse- drawn litter.

During this time much better roads were built so carriages became more and more popular. By 1605 there were traffic jams in London causing the government of the day to start thinking of a tax on these vehicles, (which was then introduced in 1637).

In Germany around 1660 a carriage called the Berlin was developed which carried four people with the coachman sitting above the front wheels.

This design became very popular and was built under license by other companies in Europe. Twenty years later the canvas blinds on the windows were replaced with glass and the first simple suspension was introduced consisting of leather straps from which the body of the carriage was suspended. The Germans then fitted curved metal springs to the Berlin which absorbed the shocks more effectively.

Around this time a two-wheeled variety was developed called the gig. This carried two people with a single horse. It was first used in Paris and was then widely adopted across Europe as the first in which to have an enjoyable fast ride.

The more sedate (wealthy) people in the large cities were carried around in sedan chairs which they hailed in same way as we do today. A sedan chair with wheels was also available, pulled by one person similar to the rickshaws of today.

They went out of fashion as the carriages were improved with new designs and more elegant characteristics. During the seventeenth century a variety of designs were developed. These included the Stagecoach and the Post Chaise. They stayed the most popular form of transport until the early twentieth century when the motorcar became the preferred form of road transport.

Sedan Chair

THE STAGECOACH

The stagecoach was introduced to Britain in the mid 17th century. It was heavy and cumbersome, drawn by four or six horses at about four miles an hour which made it vulnerable to highwaymen. The early ones had no suspension so were very uncomfortable to ride in or on top of. There were three classes of passengers the first class passengers, eight of which were packed inside in two rows of four facing each other, second class would sit in a basket attached to the rear and the third class would sit on the roof holding onto rails around the sides. When approaching a hill the second and third class passengers would have to alight from coach. Second class walked behind while the third class would help to push the carriage up the hill. The driver sat on the front above the rear of the horses with a large whip in hand to control the front horses.

Stagecoach

THE MAIL COACH

The mail coach was developed from an idea that came to John Palmer of Bath.

Wells Fargo American mail coach

He was annoyed that it took so long deliver mail between the cities of London and Bath (usually by a boy on a horse that had seen better days and took three days) that he decided to propose to the government a system whereby special coaches that would deliver mail and valuable items with armed guards, no outside passengers and pulled by good horses should be used. He encountered a lot of opposition, especially from the Post Office, which had the monopoly on the mail, but eventually won through by having the support of the Chancellor of the Exchequer (who saw it as a way of raising more taxes).The proposal was made in 1782. Two years later the first coach ran from Bath to London and was such a success that by the autumn of the following year Palmer had services running to and from sixteen more towns. By 1798 he had forty-two routes. The departure of the coaches from London at eight o'clock every evening became a social event as crowds would gather to watch them depart for all parts of the country; Swansea, Holyhead in Wales and the longest to Edinburgh, which took thirteen days with overnight stops.

That journey time was brought down to three days by the revolutionary road building of the Scotsman John Macadam, whose first trial stretch of road was in the Bristol area in 1815. It consisted of three layers of stones with the biggest at the bottom and smallest on the top with a slightly curved surface so that rainwater would run off to the side into drains. The first layer was put down and the road opened for several weeks so that the wheels of the carriages and carts would compact the stones then the next layer was added to do the same and finally the top was added to give a very solid structure. This method became known worldwide as macadamized and when tar was added to the surface to bind the stones together during the19th century it was called a tar macadam road and then became the trade name tarmac. By 1830 there were fifty-four coaches running each way between London and Manchester with a further six hundred and fifty running on other routes all over Britain.

THE POST CHAISE

This type of carriage was developed in France during the early part of the 18th century. The name meant 'pleasant seat' in French. It carried two passengers facing forward with large windows across the front and sides giving an uninterrupted view as the coachman had been replaced by two riders (called postillions) sitting on two of the four horses, usually one on the left front with the other on the right rear horse. They were luxuriously upholstered and were favoured by the wealthy citizens of the time for touring around the countryside or whilst on the Grand Tour of Europe. Fresh horses were available at every post stop so that a good speed could be sustained all day.

AMERICA

The first wagon of significance in the American west was the Conestoga which was built by German settlers in the Conestoga valley in west Pennsylvania. A number of them were acquired by George Washington to help move supplies for his army in his quest to defeat the French army near the Ohio River. They were pulled by four or six horses and were fitted with four large wide wheels which made it easier to move them over rough ground. Another special feature they had was that the bottom of the wagon was significantly lower between the front and rear axles so that the load could not move very much when travelling in the open country and it also lowered the centre of gravity making it easier to travel along the sides of hills. The roof consisted of curved wooden hoops with white canvas stretched over them reminiscent of ships' sails and they were called “Prairie Schooners”.

Conestoga wagon.

EARLY FARMING SYSTEMS

Up until the early 20th century hay making was a very arduous task using scythes to cut the crop (hay, corn, wheat or barley). The haymakers would walk in line swinging the scythe to and fro for about fifty yards then turn around, walk back and move across to start another line. When asked why they didn't carry on to the far end of the field they would reply that during the walk back they could straighten their backs. After the top surface of the crop dried it was turned over for the bottom to dry out. This was done by hand using a two pronged fork. When dry the hay would be racked into rows then lifted onto horse-drawn hay carts and made into haystacks as food for cattle during the winter months.

Hay cart

Corn, barley and wheat were gathered into bundles called sheaves which were about ten inches in diameter tied with a piece of the same crop and stood in clusters of six or eight for further drying, then later taken to the farmyard where they had a threshing machine of their own or a contractor towing a machine with a steam engine or tractor would visit the farms spending a day or two at each one. These machines separated the seeds from the stalks and filled the seed into large hessian bags which would be sold to the local miller to be ground into flour and made into bread or kept on the farm as extra food for the pigs and cattle.

Threshing machine

One sheaf was left in each field (called a policeman) to show the neighbouring villagers that the farmer hadn't finished there. Once that sheaf was removed they could enter the field to gather any seeds that were left.

Lightning Source UK Ltd.
Milton Keynes UK
UKOW02f1032131116
287527UK00001B/18/P